G000075657

From:

Date:

Message:

Inspiring
Women
Every Day

A life worth living

Mark 1:1–8

'John wore clothing made of camel's hair … and he ate locusts and wild honey.' (v.6)

Mark gives us a picture of John's clothing and diet. Consumerism has reached epic proportions in the Western world. 'Shop 'til you drop' is considered a fun occupation. Shopping malls have been likened to today's cathedrals, where people worship the god of money and possessions. As you begin this new year think of ways you can resist the siren call of consumerism and simplify your lifestyle.

1 January

Here's to the New Year!

Psalm 100

'For the LORD is good and his love endures for ever; his faithfulness continues through all generations.' (v.5)

Today, 'Worship the LORD with gladness; come before him with joyful songs' (v.2). He's brought you through another year and will see you through the next one. Celebrate His goodness and His gift of salvation with joy. We have the honour of calling the Most High God our Father and friend. That is something to celebrate and shout about. Here's to God's blessings and a righteous New Year.

31 December

Mountaintops and valleys

Mark 1:9–20

> '… he saw heaven being torn open and the Spirit descending on him like a dove.' (v.10)

This baptism experience would have been a high point for Jesus, and then, 'At once the Spirit sent him out into the desert' where He was tempted and tested. In nature, mountaintops are inevitably followed by valleys. Spiritually, this was true for Jesus and it will be true for us too. Some people have seen visions of Christ and of heaven, but most of us 'live by faith, not by sight' (2 Cor. 5:7).

2 January

Godly living in the real world

1 Peter 4:1–11

'They think it strange that you do not plunge with them into the same flood of dissipation ... ' (v.4)

It is a constant test of faith that Christians still have to live in the real world with all its challenges. We all have to make choices on how we live out our faith. And those choices impact the way other people view us. When I became a Christian, I had to make some decisions regarding my lifestyle and the company I was keeping. Let us look to the New Year with a determination to live righteously.

30 December

Communication gap

John 1:1–18

'The Word became flesh and made his dwelling among us.' (v.14)

How could the ineffable Almighty God communicate Himself to mankind's finite understanding? Nature displays the glory of God (Psa. 19:1–4; Rom. 1:20) and He spoke through prophets and miracles in Old Testament times. But we still didn't get the message. Jesus, the Word, squeezed Himself into human form – God's communication to us. Why? Because God's heart burns with the desire to bridge the communication gap.

3 January

The full armour of God

Ephesians 6:10–18

'Put on the full armour of God so that you can take your stand against the devil's schemes.' (v.11)

This coming year, set your heart towards the things of heaven and be clothed in the full armour of God. One of the best ways of deepening our faith is by being part of a Bible or home fellowship group. I go to a cell church and it's made an outstanding difference to my faith. Being part of a group encourages and nurtures one's faith in a way that's not achievable with weekly services alone.

29 December

God become man

John 1:1–2,14,18

'In the beginning was the Word, and the Word was with God, and the Word was God. He was with God in the beginning … The Word became flesh and made his dwelling among us. We have seen his glory, the glory of the One and Only [Son], who came from the Father, full of grace and truth … No-one has ever seen God, but God the One and Only [Son], who is at the Father's side, has made him known.'

4 January

Knowing God

Ephesians 3:14–20

'Now to him who is able to do immeasurably more than all we ask or imagine, according to his power ...' (v.20)

A good starting point to knowing God is reading the Bible. It is a testimony of God's character and His love for us. With knowledge comes wisdom and guidance for every area of your life. And what about the Holy Spirit? Is His voice discernible to you? There's a lot of talk about the Holy Spirit being a Person but the truth is that few Christians actually engage in a dynamic relationship with Him.

28 December

Who is this man?

Mark 1:21–45

'… a man … possessed by an evil spirit cried out, "… I know who you are – the Holy One of God!"' (vv.23–24)

The people flocked to hear Jesus' teaching and see the miracles. He was the hottest news in town, but no one guessed He was the long-awaited Messiah. Many Jews hoped for a king who would liberate them from the Roman boot. Jesus came to liberate from a very different enemy. It's ironic that the only ones who truly recognised Jesus at this stage in His ministry were the demons!

5 January

A hope and a future

Habakkuk 2:2–4

'Write down the revelation and make it plain on tablets
so that a herald may run with it.' (v.2)

The Bible urges us to write down the secret dreams and desires that God has placed in our hearts. With the New Year only four days away, start thinking of feasible changes you would like to make in your life. Ask the Holy Spirit to reveal God's plans for you this coming year. Write down your desires and start making steps towards their fulfilment. Then thank Him for His plans to give you a hope and a future.

27 December

Faith-stretching friends

Mark 2:1–17

'While Jesus was having dinner at Levi's house, many tax collectors and "sinners" were eating with him …' (v.15)

Jesus, always the radical, adds another dimension to the choice of who we spend time with. In His culture sharing a meal was a sign of friendship and He often ate with 'undesirables'. Stimulating Christian friends are a great bonus from God, but we obviously need to have non-Christian friends, otherwise the Christian community will become ghetto-like, and no one will hear the gospel.

6 January

God so loved

John 3:13–17

'No-one has ever gone into heaven except the one who came from heaven – the Son of Man. Just as Moses lifted up the snake in the desert, so the Son of Man must be lifted up, that everyone who believes in him may have eternal life. For God so loved the world that he gave his one and only Son, that whoever believes in him shall not perish but have eternal life. For God did not send his Son into the world to condemn the world, but to save the world through him.'

26 December

Rules, rules and more rules!

Mark 2:18–3:6

'He looked round at them in anger … deeply distressed at their stubborn hearts …' (3:5)

At first glance the Pharisees would be any church leader's dream congregation – avid, obedient Bible students. But the very commandments that should have brought them closer to God forged an ever-thickening barrier between them. What went wrong? They were locked in by rules and pride and their lack of humility robbed them of the wisdom to rightly interpret the Scriptures (2 Tim. 2:14–15).

Merry Christmas!

Luke 2:1–14

'Today in the town of David a Saviour has been born to you; he is Christ the Lord.' (v.11)

Christmas Day! The first Christmas was celebrated on 25 December 336 after Emperor Constantine declared Christianity the empire's favoured religion and it's been celebrated on that date by most Christians around the world ever since. So lift up your eyes and together with millions of fellow Christians around the world, celebrate the birth of the Shepherd of mankind: Jesus Christ, Lord and Saviour.

25 December

I choose you!

Mark 3:7–34

'He appointed twelve … that they might be with him and that he might send them out …' (vv.14–15)

Being chosen is a thrill; whether on the netball team, landing a much-desired job or becoming someone's life partner. The fact that out of all other 'contestants' you're 'The One', makes you feel special, honoured. Jesus chose the disciples to be His special companions and to learn how to minister to others. How will you respond today to God who reaches out to choose you to know Him better and to serve Him?

True love, not just for Christmas

1 Thessalonians 3:6–13

'May the Lord make your love increase and overflow for each other and for everyone else, just as ours does for you.' (v.12)

Paul's prayer for the church was not for an earthly, fleshly love that seeks for itself only. It was for a godly love that operates outside of itself and seeks the good of others in the midst of severe persecution and trial (vv.7,12). How about reaching out and picking up the telephone or writing an email or letter to someone who has hurt you or let you down and seek reconciliation. That is Christlike love.

24 December

Weeds, brambles, thistles

Mark 4:1–34

'Then Jesus said, "He who has ears to hear, let him hear."' (v.9)

I want to be one who bears fruit, preferably 100-fold. But that means whenever I hear or read God's Word I have to completely accept it, take it into my life and let it do its work – just as a seed has to yield fully to the earth to bring life and growth. Do not allow into your heart weeds of worry, brambles of materialism, or thistles of self-will which all choke the pure truth.

Gift-giving at Christmas

Romans 6:23

'For the wages of sin is death, but the gift of God is eternal life in Christ Jesus our Lord.' (v.23)

In Jesus Christ, we have the greatest gift anyone could ever have; the gift of eternal life. A non-perishable gift that will endure without end, without a returns policy and with unlimited guarantee of God's faithfulness to us. In Christ Jesus, God has given us Himself not just at Christmas; but for all eternity. Just like our salvation. I can't think of a better gift. Can you?

23 December

Magnificent Majesty

Revelation 19: 11 – 16

*'On his robe and on his thigh he has this name written:
KING OF KINGS AND LORD OF LORDS' (v.16)*

Jesus is still on the throne. He cannot be toppled
by military might or intellectual argument. His
powers are not diminished by old age or illness.
His policies are always relevant and beneficial to His
subjects. Make a list of your concerns, however small
or large. Then write alongside it 'He is LORD of LORDS
and KING of KINGS'. When you're tempted to be anxious,
focus again on who He is.

Unconditional love

1 Corinthians 13:1–13

'And now these three remain: faith, hope and love. But the greatest of these is love.' (v.13)

Christmas is about God's pure love for man. It is a reminder of what Christ gave up in heaven just so He could save us. And more than anything else, it is a time to put our focus back on Jesus and the great work He did while on earth. I usually think about Jesus as a last resort but I'm learning that it's best to seek the Lord's counsel first. Then I can display Christlike love to others.

22 December

All hail King Jesus

Revelation 19: 11 – 13,16

'I saw heaven standing open and there before me was a white horse, whose rider is called Faithful and True … His eyes are like blazing fire, and on his head are many crowns. He has a name written on him that no-one knows but he himself. He is dressed in a robe dipped in blood, and his name is the Word of God … On his robe and on his thigh he has this name written: KING OF KINGS AND LORD OF LORDS.'

11 January

A thoroughly good breed

Matthew 1:1–17

'A record of the genealogy of Jesus Christ the son of David, the son of Abraham …' (v.1)

In some cultures, one's genealogy determines one's station in life. It dictates where you live, your education, the person you marry, even the way you're buried. Jesus' human genealogy was pretty much a mixed one. Not many 'saviours' can confess to having a murderer (King David) and a prostitute (Rahab) as ancestors! Jesus' life wasn't dictated by His lineage. It was dictated and directed by God.

21 December

The King in action!

Mark 4:35–5:43

'At once Jesus realised that power had gone out from him.' (5:30)

Four hopeless situations: an overwhelming storm, a deranged man, an incurable illness and a dead girl. They'd tried everything to remedy each situation – frantic rowing, chains, doctors and more doctors. The problems were relentlessly moving towards their inevitable conclusion – death. But Jesus is the Lord of life (John 5:21). He brought about cataclysmic reversals. '… with God all things are possible' (Matt. 19:25–26).

12 January

The persecuted Church

Luke 2:21–40

*'This child is destined to cause the falling and rising of
many in Israel ... ' (v.34)*

Many have lost their lives because they
have chosen to follow Christ. Others have
lost their homes, businesses and families
because of whom they chose to serve; but what joy for
these people when they see their Saviour face to face
in heaven! Today we salute the persecuted Christians
and pray for them and their families and those the
imprisoned and the martyred leave behind. They have
not believed in vain.

Faith's building blocks

Mark 6:1–52

'They were completely amazed, for they had not understood … their hearts were hardened.' (vv.51–52)

I n teaching it is imperative to build new information onto previous understanding. I use God's past faithfulness to anchor me and make my heart ready for the next step. Try keeping a journal for a month. Reading back over the past encourages me to trust Him for the present. Note down verses that speak to you, answers to prayer, what you're learning about God. I guarantee reviewing it will build your faith.

13 January

Do not worry

Matthew 6:31–34

'So do not worry, saying, "What shall we eat?" or "What shall we drink?" or "What shall we wear?" For the pagans run after all these things, and your heavenly Father knows that you need them. But seek first his kingdom and his righteousness, and all these things will be given to you as well. Therefore do not worry about tomorrow, for tomorrow will worry about itself. Each day has enough trouble of its own.'

19 December

Truth versus tradition

Mark 6:53–7:30

'You have let go of the commands of God and are holding on to the traditions of men.' (7:8)

Identifying which are God's commands and which are man's traditions is essential. Holding all the commandments in balance is tricky. Sharing the gospel with work colleagues is really important, but not during the working day – that's robbing our employer. Meeting others' needs is vital, but not at the expense of our family or even our own health. We may have to say 'no' and sometimes that's hard.

14 January

God will provide

Matthew 6:25–34

'But seek first his kingdom and his righteousness, and all these things will be given to you as well.' (v.33)

As you frantically race through your Christmas 'to do' list this weekend, spare a thought for those in need. There are many people around the world who cannot celebrate Christmas with a king-size turkey and presents to match. They do not even have enough to eat. Or perhaps you too are wondering where your next meal is coming from. Take heart from words from the King Himself that God will provide.

18 December

The personal touch

Mark 7:31–8:26

'He took the blind man by the hand and led him outside the village.' (8:23)

Jesus models a one-by-one approach to people. God has a personal touch in all His dealings with us. Time is no problem to Him, so He doesn't have a 'to do list' of things to accomplish today. That means He can be totally flexible and always has time to listen to any one of His children who happens to want to spend time with Him. What a relief to discover He is not stressed or busy, nor does He have a full diary!

Jesus, the King

Isaiah 9:1–7

'Of the increase of his government and peace there will be no end.' (v.7)

It's reassuring to know that faith in Jesus is not dependent on external forces, as they're dynamic and thus subject to change – unlike God who is unchanging. A saving knowledge of Jesus Christ brings unshakeable peace and will equip us with the strength to deal with life's hardships. Pray for peace for all men and for the government in your country to know the peace of Christ.

17 December

Get the full story

Mark 8:27–9:13

'… the Son of Man must suffer many things and be
rejected … he must be killed …' (8:31)

This shocking news sent the disciples into denial.
They had no place in their belief system for a
Messiah who would suffer and die. It's so easy
to focus on the pleasant bits of being a Christian. But
this is only half the story. Some people today can't
get their heads around the fact that being a Christian
involves suffering. Jesus pointed out that self-denial
and cross-bearing are involved in following Him.

16 January

With eyes focused on heaven

John 3: 13–17

'No-one has ever gone into heaven except the one who came from heaven – the Son of Man.' (v.13)

Our faith is the only one with a God who reaches out to the cesspit of humanity to say, 'Whatever you do will never be good enough to impress Me because of your sin and because I am holy, I cannot abide sin. Tell you what, I'll come down to earth as a man, make Myself sin personified and redeem you in the process. All you have to do is acknowledge your sin and accept that I, Jesus, am mankind's only hope.'

16 December

Man of Sorrows

Isaiah 53:1–12

'He was despised and rejected by men, a man of sorrows, and familiar with suffering' (v.3)

Jesus' life clearly showed that pain is part of our human condition. We can either grow through it and allow the fruit of the Spirit to be developed in us, or we can resist it and become stunted and bitter. Do you have sorrow in your heart? Jesus has been there. Maybe not in the exact circumstances, but He is intimately acquainted with sorrow. He knows your pain and can walk through it with you if you let Him.

17 January

A thoroughly humble beginning!

Luke 2:1–20

'… and she gave birth … and placed him in a manger, because there was no room for them in the inn.' (v.7)

Two thousand years later, we are still celebrating the Saviour's birth, but we've become so familiar with it, we stand in danger of missing its relevance to our lives. This Advent, let us look forward to Christmas with joy not familiarity. Celebrate the Saviour's birth with a renewed passion and endeavour to have a Christ-focused Christmas. Remember He's the reason for the season.

15 December

The Suffering Messiah

Isaiah 53:3–5

'He was despised and rejected by men, a man of sorrows, and familiar with suffering … he was despised, and we esteemed him not. Surely he took up our infirmities and carried our sorrows, yet we considered him stricken by God, smitten by him, and afflicted. But he was pierced for our transgressions, he was crushed for our iniquities; the punishment that brought us peace was upon him, and by his wounds we are healed.'

18 January

Jesus, the God–Man

Luke 1:26–38

'The Holy Spirit will come upon you … So the holy one to be born will be called the Son of God.' (v.35)

Christ's conception is incomprehensible to the human mind but perfectly in line with the workings of a miraculous, limitless God. Jesus, the God–Man. Jesus, our Saviour. Jesus, the One who understands and identifies with life on earth. Spend some time rejoicing in having a Saviour who understands that life on earth is not easy but who works everything out for His own glory and your own good.

14 December

St Stephens or City Temple?

Mark 9: 14–50

'… "we saw a man driving out demons in your name and we told him to stop, because he was not one of us."' (v.38)

Jesus' disciples thought they were pretty important – the 'in-crowd'. They chose to say, 'You're not part of our group, therefore you're wrong, so you can't do it.' Church history is littered with similar situations. Jesus' response illustrates a far more inclusive attitude than that of His disciples. He urged them to embrace those who were working in His name. How is your group? Are you inclusive to new people?

19 January

Re-examining Christianity

Isaiah 40:3–5

'And the glory of the Lord will be revealed, and all mankind together will see it.' (v.5)

The Christian faith defies all logic. It is based on a God–Man whose conception, humble birth and horrifying death are so fantastic one has two choices; to believe that Jesus is who He says He is – or not. He frees us from the shackles of good works and enables us to live a life of freedom before God. Christmas is the best time to re-examine our faith as it reminds us of the real reason Jesus came to earth.

13 December

Find one thin camel!

Mark 10:1–31

'… a man ran up to [Jesus] and fell on his knees before him. "Good teacher … what must I do to inherit eternal life?" ' (v.17)

Jesus points out the absurdity of the question that mere religion is unable to answer. Find one very thin camel and one very large needle! No human endeavour can unlock the key to heaven (v.27a). It is bolted firmly shut against such paltry efforts. We are hopeless and helpless and the sooner we admit it, the better. However, the grace of God responds exuberantly to hopeless and helpless people (v.27b).

20 January

We believe

1 Thessalonians 4:14–16

'We believe that Jesus died and rose again and so we believe that God will bring with Jesus those who have fallen asleep in him. According to the Lord's own word, we tell you that we who are still alive, who are left till the coming of the Lord, will certainly not precede those who have fallen asleep. For the Lord himself will come down from heaven, with a loud command, with the voice of the archangel and with the trumpet call of God, and the dead in Christ will rise first.'

12 December

Passionate prayer

Mark 10:32–52

'Many rebuked him and told him to be quiet, but he shouted all the more, "Son of David, have mercy on me!"' (v.48)

Hope surged. Jesus the Healer was coming along this very road where Bartimaeus had lingered for days on end. He struggled to get his mind into gear. He began to cry out: 'Jesus, it's me, have mercy!' His desperation gave impetus to his vocal cords. The cry became a yell. The yell became a bellow: 'Jesus, mercy!' Moments later his world changed forever for Jesus responded to his passionate prayer.

21 January

He's coming back!

1 Thessalonians 4:13–18

'For the Lord himself will come down from heaven …' (v.16)

Christianity is a faith that challenges us to look at our human weaknesses without guilt and condemnation. It's reassuring to know that our faith is not one based on good works or bonus points. It is a faith that does not shy away from the hard issues of life but instead exhorts us to look at the larger picture; we are only on earth for a while and Jesus is coming back for His Church.

11 December

Long live the King!

Mark 11:1–33

'When they brought the colt to Jesus … he sat on it … He overturned the tables of the money changers …' (vv.7,15)

Jesus was effectively saying, 'If you say I'm your King, then you must be prepared for Me to upset your lifestyle. Changes will need to be made to restore the Temple to what My Father intended it to be.' He says the same thing to us today. If we say He is our God and King, then we need to do what He says (Matt. 7:21). This will indeed upset our lifestyle as it is examined in the light of His piercing kingly gaze.

22 January

What second coming?

Revelation 22:7; 2 Peter 3:10–12

'Behold, I am coming soon! Blessed is he who keeps the words of the prophecy in this book.' (v.7)

The Middle Age Church used Advent to prepare for the second coming in much the same way as we would dedicate a set time to 'the things of the Lord'. All through the centuries people have mocked our faith, declaring, 'Where is this "coming" he promised?' (2 Pet. 3:4). Let's live each day full of hope and deep conviction of our faith and, above all, let us live each day full of holy expectation.

10 December

Do what it says

Mark 12:1–44

'Jesus replied, "Are you not in error because you do not know the Scriptures or the power of God?"' (v.24)

The religious leaders had a thorough knowledge of Scripture, but this didn't serve them well. They were meticulous in obeying certain parts of it but really lost the plot when it came to humility, love and mercy. They had become proud in their academic knowledge. A humble widow put into practice what she knew of God's Word. She may not have known very much, but what she did know she obeyed. Let's follow her example.

23 January

A just God?

Psalm 73:1–22

'But as for me … I envied the arrogant when I saw the prosperity of the wicked.' (vv.2–3)

We understand that God's ways are infinitely higher than our ways but that does not make the prosperity of the wicked any less palatable. This psalm is a cry from a man after God's heart but it could easily be a psalm from anybody's heart. The psalmist shows us what we are expected to do in such situations: '[enter] the sanctuary of God'. With meditation and reflection comes understanding.

9 December

Author par excellence

'Let us fix our eyes on Jesus, the author and perfecter of our faith …' (v.2).

An author writes a book. The reader receives it as a finished work. So it is with Jesus. He created salvation. We can add nothing to His sacrifice (Heb. 10: 14). He alone made it possible for us to escape judgment and be welcomed into the presence of a holy God (Rom. 6:23). If your race feels a bit uphill at the moment, or you've wandered off the racecourse, fix your eyes on Jesus the author par excellence.

24 January

Faith or fake?

John 15:1–8

> *'… while every branch that does bear fruit he prunes so that it will be even more fruitful.' (v.2)*

The Church in the Middle Ages wasn't perfect but I believe they have a lot to teach this generation about tenacity, discipline and consistent faith in God. Today, let us look back with thanks to those people who laid the foundations for a rich heritage in Christian tradition that we still celebrate today. What kind of spiritual heritage are you leaving for your loved ones – faith or fake?

8 December

Perfecter of our faith

Hebrews 12:2–4

'Let us fix our eyes on Jesus, the author and perfecter of our faith, who for the joy set before him endured the cross, scorning its shame, and sat down at the right hand of the throne of God. Consider him who endured such opposition from sinful men, so that you will not grow weary and lose heart. In your struggle against sin, you have not yet resisted to the point of shedding your blood.'

25 January

Looking towards Jesus

Luke 3:21–22; 4:1–15

'… where for forty days he was tempted by the devil.' (4:2)

Advent is a reminder of our new life in Jesus. Some find fasting helpful spiritually. Fasting causes us to look above and towards Him. Maybe you have never fasted or even observed Advent. I doubt you're the only one. In a bid to move with the times and away from 'dead' traditions, Christians are in danger of forsaking Advent and its rich spiritual roots. This year, celebrate Advent the way it was meant to be done, with piety and reverential joy.

7 December

Don't panic!

Mark 13:1–37

'When you hear of wars and rumours of wars, do not be alarmed. Such things must happen … Watch!' (vv.7,37)

Jesus says, 'Don't be alarmed.' Why not? Famines, wars and persecution sound ghastly enough for anyone to be fearful. The reassurance in verse 32 puts it into context. God knows the timetable. The universe is not out of control. God is still on His throne (Rev. 4:2). So, instead of worrying about what the world's coming to, we should put our energies into being on guard, keeping watch, being alert.

26 January

A thorough cleansing

Romans 8:1–17

'… but the mind controlled by the Spirit is life and peace …' (v.6)

Where we have failed, remember the Father gave up His only Son to cleanse us of our sins. Where we have been disappointed, let us continue to hold on to the one Person who will not let us down; Jesus. The storms of life will always come but we have the Holy Spirit residing inside us and using the storms to mould us into the person He wants us to be. His desires are possible, feasible and achievable.

6 December

Nothing held back

Mark 14:1–42

'She has done a beautiful thing to me … She poured perfume on my body beforehand to prepare for my burial.' (vv.6,8)

The broken jar is a powerful symbol of total consecration. None of the perfume was kept for another time – it was all poured out, and the aroma billowed silently into the room. Everyone knew what Mary had done. Lives that are poured out in worship and service for God will also have a significant effect on those around them. Similarly people will see Jesus in us if we walk closely with Him.

27 January

Renewing our strength

Isaiah 40:28–31

'Do you not know? Have you not heard? The LORD is the everlasting God, the Creator of the ends of the earth. He will not grow tired or weary, and his understanding no-one can fathom. He gives strength to the weary and increases the power of the weak. Even youths grow tired and weary, and young men stumble and fall; but those who hope in the LORD will renew their strength. They will soar on wings like eagles; they will run and not grow weary, they will walk and not be faint.'

5 December

Religious fervour gone crazy

Mark 14:43–72

'Then some began to spit at him; they blindfolded him, struck him with their fists, and said, "Prophesy!"' (v.65)

Religious fervour is a highly volatile emotion. Unchecked and unguided it can lead to ghastly situations, even in today's Church. Division over doctrine unleashes the beast within. Well-meaning, godly people lash out with invective and angry gestures. But there is never any excuse for unchristian behaviour. We need to plead for the Holy Spirit to give wisdom and to build the fruit of self-control into our lives.

28 January

Strength to face the day

Isaiah 40:18–31

'… those who hope in the LORD will renew their strength.' (v.31)

Hard to believe, but the early Christians faced exactly the same situations we face today. The Roman Empire exhibited a similar moral deficit. In fact, it was probably worse. In addition, Christians faced death for their assertion that Jesus was the only true God and they would worship no other, least of all the Emperor. They persisted, thrived and spread the gospel in the face of severe persecution.

4 December

Mission accomplished

Mark 15:1–47

'With a loud cry, Jesus breathed his last. The curtain of the temple was torn in two from top to bottom.'
(vv.37–38)

It's hard for us who live this side of the cross to understand what a turnaround this was in people's thinking and understanding about God. He had always been untouchable and unapproachable except by an exclusive band of people using special rituals. Suddenly this God now becomes accessible. By His death Jesus has paid the price for our sin, so no more sacrifice is necessary. Let's not abuse that privilege.

29 January

Reflection or introspection

Psalm 131

*'But I have stilled and quietened my soul;
like a weaned child with its mother ... is my soul
within me.' (v.2)*

A still and quiet soul understands the difference between healthy reflection and guilty introspection. One operates in the freedom of childlike trust, while the other operates in spiritual bondage. As Christians, it's important we understand the difference between the two so that we enjoy our faith and share it with others, rather than living a life of works and being miserable because of it.

3 December

Unbelievable news!

Mark 16:1–20

'He has risen! … "He is going ahead of you into Galilee. There you will see him, just as he told you."'
(vv.6–7)

Maybe they were in shock at seeing Him die so horribly. Whatever the disciples' reasons, Jesus was clearly disappointed at their lack of faith. But He didn't give up on them. He forgave them and commissioned them to take His message to the world. At times when our faith is stretched to the uttermost, let's take special care to remember what Jesus has said and build our faith on His Word.

30 January

What use hope?

Romans 8:18–25

'For in this hope we were saved … But if we hope for what we do not yet have, we wait for it patiently.'
(vv.24–25)

Although visibly unseen, God is right beside us. Our hope in God will produce a visible quality in our character that Jesus Himself exhibits with us: patience and longsuffering. Women can juggle 50 things at the same time but we expend far too much energy lamenting on our shortcomings. Be merciful with yourself and remember that it is in Christ we put our hope not in our own strength.

2 December

Friendship and forgiveness

Genesis 2: 18–24

'The LORD God said, "It is not good for the man to be alone. I will make a helper suitable for him."' (v.18)

Friendship is a deep human need. Many Bible stories reflect this need, from God giving Adam a companion, to the friendships made amongst the first evangelists, Paul, Luke, Lydia and so on. Our Lord Jesus also had friends – Mary, Martha and Lazarus who lived in Bethany, as well as the disciples and their families. No man – or woman – can live a rounded and fulfilled life without the fun and interaction of friends.

31 January

Revisiting Advent

Leviticus 16:2–21

'He is to … confess over it … all their sins – and put them on the goat's head.' (v.21)

As we approach Christmas with advertisers' hard-to-resist urgings to spend, spend, spend, let's bear in mind the real meaning of Christmas; the celebration of the birth of the Saviour who became sin, so that through Him everyone who believes in Him would have eternal life. As we embark on our Christmas shopping trips, let us remember the millions of people who have yet to be given the greatest gift of all: the saving knowledge of Jesus Christ.

1 December

A companion

Genesis 2:19,21–22

'The LORD God said, "It is not good for the man to be alone. I will make a helper suitable for him."… So the LORD God caused the man to fall into a deep sleep; and while he was sleeping, he took one of the man's ribs and closed up the place with flesh. Then the LORD God made a woman from the rib he had taken out of the man, and he brought her to the man.'

Fly like the eagles

Psalm 40

'*… may your love and your truth always protect me.*' *(v.11)*

By developing a consciousness of the presence of the living God and by always trusting in Him in good times or bad, you will be enabled to fly like the eagles, thus seeing things in their right perspective. God has given us treasures of darkness for a specific reason: in order that we may know that it is He who calls us by name and that the greatest treasure is growth in relationship with Him.

30 November

Best friends

Ruth 1:1–10,16–18

'Where you go I will go … Your people will be my people and your God my God.' (v.16)

The Bible has several accounts of close friendships, such as David and Jonathan, Jesus with His 'beloved disciple' and also Lazarus, but perhaps none are so completely recorded as the bond of friendship between Naomi and Ruth. Their friendship crossed the barriers of age and race in a culture where different tribes did not mix. They shared when times were good and when they had nothing. True friends.

2 February

From darkness to light

Psalm 118:1–24

'The stone the builders rejected has become the capstone ...' (v.22)

Nothing could have been more devastating than the death of Jesus on the cross, and yet, there is nothing more triumphant than His resurrection from the dead. If we put our faith in God in the midst of our suffering then we will step from the darkness of despair into the glorious light of His love. Our own stones of darkness, rejection and pain can become new building blocks in our life of faith.

29 November

Like-minded friends

Acts 18: 1–3,18–26

*'… because he was a tentmaker as they were, he
stayed and worked with them.' (v.3)*

The blessing of having like-minded friends
is priceless – those who understand our
situation or problems because they have close
knowledge of our gifts and capabilities, as well as our
weaknesses! We can be confident that their advice is
genuine. Painting and sketching, quilting, tent-making,
whatever the shared skill, the greatest bond is the
bond of shared faith and being able to pray together.

3 February

New every morning

Lamentations 3:19–26

'I remember my affliction and my wandering, the bitterness and the gall. I well remember them, and my soul is downcast within me. Yet this I call to mind and therefore I have hope: Because of the LORD's great love we are not consumed, for his compassions never fail. They are new every morning; great is your faithfulness. I say to myself, "The LORD is my portion; therefore I will wait for him." The LORD is good to those whose hope is in him, to the one who seeks him; it is good to wait quietly for the salvation of the LORD.'

28 November

Supportive friends

Acts 21:7–16

'Some of the disciples from Caesarea accompanied us and brought us to the home of Mnason, where we were to stay.' (v.16)

Jesus was acutely aware of people's need of companionship; remember how He sent out His disciples in twos. And Luke shows us in Acts how the first Christians regularly met together, travelled together and stayed in each other's homes. It was their contact, prayer-cell and mission-base. Our need today for prayer cells, encouragement and help in time of stress is just as vital.

4 February

Hope of relief

Lamentations 3:13–26

'Yet this I call to mind and therefore I have hope' (v. 21)

Lamentations is the most melancholic book of the Prophets. The author was completely overwhelmed by the destruction of Jerusalem, the sin that caused it and the consequent suffering. Perhaps your life feels similar? Yet in the midst of the 'heaviness' of Lamentations, is one of the most uplifting passages in the whole Bible! God's compassion never fails and therefore we can have hope. Great is His faithfulness!

27 November

A friend's invitation

John 1:43–50

' "Come and see," said Philip.' (v.46)

Philip didn't give up when confronted by Nathanael's negativism – he made the life-changing invitation. Many things we do and places we go, are motivated or suggested by our friends. Sometimes I have grudgingly accepted an invitation and then have been thrilled by the outcome. Just as Jesus knew all about Nathanael, He knows all about us too. So, let's be open to invitations and opportunities offered by our friends.

5 February

Making a choice

Proverbs 9: 12– 18

'If you are wise, your wisdom will reward you …' (v.12)

Both wisdom and folly have a house to which mankind is invited. Although wisdom's invitation (9:4) and folly's invitation (9:16) appear similar, they are in consequence very different. Folly is seductive; and a woman of deception and trickery. When you are in despair or struggling, which woman do you listen to? The fear of the Lord leads us through the door of wisdom rather than down the dark alley of folly.

A helping hand

Nehemiah 12:40–43

'The two choirs that gave thanks then took their places … so did I … ' (v.40)

After my husband died, I stopped singing solos in church. On one occasion, a friend came up beside me, took my hand and gently said: 'We'll do it together.' We sang 'Blessed Assurance' with everyone joining in the chorus. Something that I could not have done on my own was made possible because Jean was there to give me a helping hand. She encouraged me back to doing something for God that He had gifted me to do.

6 February

Learning about life

Proverbs 9:1–12

'Wisdom has built her house; she has hewn out its seven pillars.' (v.1)

Wisdom is depicted in Proverbs as a woman who, in these verses, invites you to a lush banquet. Selwyn Hughes describes the seven pillars as: 1. Trust; 2. Integrity; 3. Generosity; 4. Diligence; 5. Watchfulness with words; 6. Friendship; 7. Personal purity. How strong are your pillars? If wisdom were to invite you to strengthen your pillars what might she say to you in each of these areas?

25 November

The place of friendship

Proverbs 17:9– 17

'A friend loves at all times, and a brother is born for adversity.' (v.17)

Most friends are occasional acquaintances whilst others seem to become the once-a-year variety on the Christmas card list, but we can thank God for those friends to whom we can turn at any time and know that they will do their best for us. Have you ever thought of Jesus as your friend? Take time out to remember that Jesus called His disciples His friends, and how He loves at all times.

7 February

Guarding our hearts

Proverbs 4:7–27

'Above all else, guard your heart, for it is the wellspring of life.' (v.23)

I t is clear that the heart has the potential to draw us away from godly wisdom and conduct. We must guard our hearts and seek to have a purity of heart. In the Beatitudes Jesus declares: 'Blessed are the pure in heart, for they will see God' (Matt. 5:8). The more pure a person is, the clearer his or her sight of God becomes. How do we attain that purity? By fulfilling the previous conditions of the Beatitudes.

24 November

Constant love

John 15:15–17

'I no longer call you servants, because a servant does not know his master's business. Instead, I have called you friends, for everything that I learned from my Father I have made known to you. You did not choose me, but I chose you and appointed you to go and bear fruit – fruit that will last. Then the Father will give you whatever you ask in my name. This is my command: Love each other.'

8 February

Keeping the commands

Proverbs 3:1–18

*'... in all your ways acknowledge him, and he will
make your paths straight.' (v.6)*

Proverbs not only exhorts us to embrace
wisdom, but also speaks of its benefits. To
embrace wisdom is to keep God's commands
close to our hearts. The benefit is that our lives will
be prolonged and we will have inner prosperity.
Wisdom is not following our own way, but following the
path of the Lord. Have you come to rely on your own
way of doing things or do you acknowledge God in all
your ways?

23 November

Befriending the sick

Mark 2:1–12

'Some men came, bringing to him a paralytic, carried by four of them.' (v.3)

Who were those unnamed men whose gentle care has been recalled through the centuries? It would seem most probable that they were close relatives of the paralysed man, for who else would have put themselves to such bother? We don't know how far they had carried the stretcher, but we know they were determined to take their man right to Jesus' feet and that meeting with Jesus was life-changing.

9 February

Wisdom and wealth

Proverbs 2

'For the LORD gives wisdom, and from his mouth come knowledge and understanding.' (v.6)

One of the richest treasures in the darkness is the wisdom we can gain through wrestling with life's difficulties. In the midst of your more difficult times do you ask for wisdom as James 1:5 implores? Do want to grow and become wise through the experience? Or is your focus on the pain itself? One of the keys to gaining wisdom is to read wisdom! We are to saturate ourselves with God's Truth.

22 November

Befriending the sick again

Acts 3:1–10

'Now a man crippled from birth was being carried to the temple gate called Beautiful … ' (v.2)

The man crippled was 'being carried' by friends who did this every day. Most of us can look back on a time when we have needed to be 'carried' by friends. And it isn't always by our nearest and closest friends. There are times when we just need someone who knows us, someone, or a group, with whom we can feel comfortable, so that the most painful and unpleasant of experiences are made a touch easier to bear.

10 February

Choose

Joshua 24:14–16

"Now fear the LORD and serve him with all faithfulness. Throw away the gods your forefathers worshipped beyond the River and in Egypt, and serve the LORD. But if serving the LORD seems undesirable to you, then choose for yourselves this day whom you will serve, whether the gods your forefathers served beyond the River, or the gods of the Amorites, in whose land you are living. But as for me and my household, we will serve the LORD." Then the people answered, "Far be it from us to forsake the LORD to serve other gods!"

21 November

Job's comforters

Job 2: 11 – 13

'When Job's three friends … heard about all the troubles … [they] met together … to go and sympathise … ' (v.11)

Eliphaz, Bildad and Zophar were obviously well-meaning and kind people and have become known as 'Job's comforters'. They were willing to leave their own homes in order to go and support their friend Job. What a moving picture we have in verse 13 when we read: 'Then they sat on the ground with him for seven days and nights.' They were true friends, even though their conversation was no help at all!

Sincerity and truth

Joshua 24

'Now fear the LORD and serve him with all faithfulness…' (v.14)

Joshua implores the people to cling to the Lord, as it is He who fights for them. He warns them not to go back and cling to the rest of the nations, pointing out that if they do then the nations will, in fact, become a snare and a trap to them. If they are to serve the Lord God, then they must serve Him in sincerity and truth. In the difficult times, are you tempted to go back to old and familiar forms of security rather than cling to God?

20 November

Friends of the earth

Psalm 24:1–5

'The earth is the LORD's, and everything in it, the world, and all who live in it.' (v.1)

We have become familiar with the tag 'Friends of … ' whether it is related to a hospital, a theatre, church or zoo, and we recognise that some institutions would just crumble without the loyalty and dedication of their 'Friends'. It should be our natural response to put our energies into good stewardship of God's creation. We all need to be friends of this vast, breath-taking miracle – earth.

12 February

Restored to safety

*'The sacrifices of God are a broken spirit; a broken
and contrite heart …' (v.17)*

In 2 Samuel 11 we read of David's adultery with
Bathsheba. However much of a mess David made
of his life, his story is one of victory in the end,
because he understood the depth of his sin and came
to repentance. Hence he was able to write Psalm 51.
Do you feel that you need to be restored to a place
of safety? We, too, can be restored, if, like David, we
examine our hearts and truly repent.

19 November

Strangers can be friends

John 12: 12– 19

'Many people, because they had heard that he had given this miraculous sign, went out to meet him.' (v.18)

When I attended an international conference of Christian women, I knew four people out of about eleven hundred! But it didn't matter – we all felt one in Jesus and it was the most fantastic feeling. We made friends with women from Pakistan, Tonga and Chicago … we forged links with women from Australia and shared the Peace with women from South Korea. It was inspirational to be part of such a crowd.

13 February

Fighting an attack

1 John 1:5–2:25

'If we claim to have fellowship with him yet walk in the darkness, we lie and do not live by the truth.' (v.6)

Satan's means of attack are enticement, trickery and deception. In 1 Peter 5:8 we are warned: 'Your enemy the devil prowls around like a roaring lion looking for someone to devour.' Do you keep a watch out for the enemy attacking you? In relation to Satan prowling around like a lion, Peter advises us, 'Be self-controlled and alert' (1 Pet. 5:8), and 'Resist him, standing firm in the faith …' (1 Pet. 5:9).

Forgiveness

Daniel 1:3– 17

'Then the king ordered Ashpenaz, chief of his court officials, to bring in some of the Israelites from the royal family and the nobility.' (v.3)

Most of us love foreign food and travel. However, we see that for Daniel and his friends, travel meant exile, foreign food was 'unclean' and the people were dreaded enemies. I have great admiration for Daniel, Shadrach, Meshach and Abednego – they could so easily have become drawn into a spiral of hate against their Babylonian captors but, instead, they began their new life in a spirit of forgiveness.

14 February

Putting on the armour

Ephesians 6

'Put on the full armour of God so that you can take your stand against the devil's schemes.' (v.11)

One of the means that God has given us to stay 'covered' is the armour of God. We no longer have to offer physical sacrifices but we do have to put on God's invisible armour. We must not miss out a single chink of the armour, but be covered from head to foot. Notice the word full. If you do put on the armour each day, do you put on the full armour; or do you try to get by with just part of the armour?

17 November

'We also forgive everyone'

Luke 11:1–4

'One day Jesus was praying in a certain place. When he finished, one of his disciples said to him, "Lord, teach us to pray, just as John taught his disciples." He said to them, "When you pray, say: "'Father, hallowed be your name, your kingdom come. Give us each day our daily bread. Forgive us our sins, for we also forgive everyone who sins against us. And lead us not into temptation.'"'

15 February

Covering is crucial

Psalm 91

'He will cover you with his feathers, and under his wings you will find refuge ...' (v.4)

'Covering' speaks of security, safety and protection. In New Testament terms, to be 'covered' means to be 'in Christ', and that is our place of safety. In Greek, to believe in Christ involves a verb of action, so when we believe in Christ we believe into Christ. Our faith carries us into Him. To be in Christ is to be covered by what He is: holiness, righteousness and purity.

16 November

All need to be forgiven

Romans 3:21–26

'... for all have sinned and fall short of the glory of God ...' (v.23)

Paul's stark words could not be more succinct. We have all sinned. We all fall short of how we know we ought to behave. But our sins, which would have damned us to our own personal hell, have been wiped away through the death of our Lord and Saviour Jesus Christ. He has paid the price of our sin – whatever it is – and by committing our lives to Him, we can be reconciled to our Creator God.

16 February

Protection and peace

Psalm 29

'The LORD gives strength to his people; the LORD blesses his people with peace.' (v.11)

God does protect us when we ask, but there are spiritual principles that we must carry out for our own protection. These put us in a safe place, but it is Satan's objective to draw us out of our place of safety. Our hearts and minds are particularly vulnerable to attack. We must recognise the battle and take steps to seek protection and then we will have deep peace that passes all understanding (Phil.4:7)

15 November

Our need of forgiveness

Psalm 51:1–10

'Against you, you only, have I sinned and done what is evil in your sight … ' (v.4)

This is the psalm where King David is pouring out his contrite heart to God following his adultery with the beautiful Bathsheba. He may have been a brilliant military tactician and an inspired poet, but he was transparently flawed. We are all flawed and have dark secrets hidden away of which we are bitterly ashamed. Whatever we have done, our God is merciful and waits to forgive each one who truly repents.

17 February

Seeking and finding

1 Chronicles 28:8–9

'So now I charge you in the sight of all Israel and of the assembly of the LORD, and in the hearing of our God: Be careful to follow all the commands of the LORD your God, that you may possess this good land and pass it on as an inheritance to your descendants for ever. And you, my son Solomon, acknowledge the God of your father, and serve him with wholehearted devotion and with a willing mind, for the LORD searches every heart and understands every motive behind the thoughts. If you seek him, he will be found by you; but if you forsake him, he will reject you for ever.'

14 November

The second chance

John 21:15–19

'Jesus said to Simon Peter, "Simon son of John, do you truly love me more than these?"' (v.15)

Peter was the spontaneous character renowned both for his outburst of faith at Caesarea Philippi and his deliberate denial of Jesus. We can all find reflections of our own behaviour in Peter. Yet Jesus loved him despite his faults. Jesus gives a simple example of true forgiveness. He didn't trawl back over the past, He just asked where Peter stood at that particular moment, and then gave him a mission.

18 February

Wholehearted devotion

1 Chronicles 28

'… serve him with wholehearted devotion …' (v.9)

We are called to seek God with our whole heart. What comes across strongly in 1 Chronicles is that when God's people obey, God blesses them. When they disobey, God cancels their spiritual privileges. The message is clear – we must be faithful to God! How often do you stop to recall the fact that God searches your heart and knows your motives? In what way might some of your motives not have been right?

Forgiving each other

James 5:13–16,19–20

*'Therefore confess your sins to each other and pray
for each other so that you may be healed.' (v.16)*

Paul underlines the importance of forgiveness
and reconciliation in 2 Corinthians 5:19–21:
'And he has committed to us the message of
reconciliation' (v.19). Is there someone in your family,
or amongst your work colleagues, with whom there
is an 'atmosphere'? Perhaps today is the day you can
be an ambassador for Christ and, by His grace, bring
apology, forgiveness, peace and reconciliation.

The profit of perseverance

James 5:7–19

'As you know, we consider blessed those who have persevered.' (v.11)

Perhaps one of the greatest 'treasures in the darkness' is our ability to develop perseverance through suffering. Romans 5:3–4 says: '… we also rejoice in our sufferings, because we know that suffering produces perseverance; perseverance, character; and character, hope.' Perseverance has a knock-on effect. Persevering is not just pushing through, but pushing through in faith and with the right attitude.

12 November

Forgiving ourselves

1 Samuel 1:3–17

'In bitterness of soul Hannah wept much and prayed to the Lord.' (v.10)

Some women feel so bitterly despondent at not being able to have children that their lives become fixated upon their loss, blaming themselves and God. I believe that a first step in coming to terms with a situation like this is to give it to God in prayer. Sometimes that prayer will be tears, sighs, screams and moans, but God is there to take away the hurt and replace it with His peace.

20 February

More than conquerors

Romans 8:28–39

'No, in all these things we are more than conquerors through him who loved us.' (v.37)

Soldiers receive information and go through hard training to equip them to conquer their enemies. We see that preparing for the battlefield requires training and discipline. What are the areas of your spiritual life in which you require greater training to be more than a conqueror through Him who loves you? Are discipline and obeying commands things that you find easy, or do you need to come to God afresh and ask His help?

11 November

Accepting God's forgiveness

Psalm 139: 1–24

'I praise you because I am fearfully and wonderfully made; your works are wonderful, I know that full well.' (v.14)

The psalmist said that we are 'fearfully and wonderfully made' and that was 3,000 years before fingerprints and DNA were discovered! Each individual is a miraculously engineered machine plus a powerhouse of complex emotions. We all make wrong decisions, some of which may have totally altered our lives but, remember, God created you, He knows and understands, and offers you loving forgiveness.

21 February

Developing inner strength

Isaiah 35

'Strengthen the feeble hands, steady the knees that
give way ...' (v.3)

Inner strength is also developed in the wilderness,
which is described in Isaiah 35. In the midst of the
dryness of the desert, blossoms begin to appear
out of nowhere. This phenomenon is the same in our
own lives – when we let go of trying to make things
work, and trust ourselves instead to the safety of
Almighty God, in the dryness of our lives, springs of
living water bring forth blossom.

God knows you

Psalm 139: 1,13,15– 16

'O LORD, you have searched me and you know me … For you created my inmost being; you knit me together in my mother's womb … My frame was not hidden from you when I was made in the secret place. When I was woven together in the depths of the earth, your eyes saw my unformed body. All the days ordained for me were written in your book before one of them came to be.'

22 February

Deep satisfaction

Jeremiah 31:23–34

'I will refresh the weary and satisfy the faint.' (v.25)

God does not speak of a temporary or superficial hope, but a deep satisfaction. Do you feel satisfied by God? In the valley do you tend to turn away and run back to a more comfortable place? Or do you allow yourself to go through the valley, even though difficult and dry, and experience first hand the faithfulness of God? It's so easy to know about His faithfulness without actually experiencing it.

9 November

Forgiving others

Colossians 3: 12– 17

'Bear with each other and forgive whatever grievances you may have against one another.' (v.13)

Paul emphasises the need for forgiveness. Forgiveness is not an optional extra – no, it is our duty to forgive because the Lord has forgiven us. All the other splendid Christian attributes are negated if we cannot come to terms with grievances. We need to ask the Lord to help us recognise where we have harboured grudges, and to soften our hearts and help us forgive as we have been forgiven.

23 February

Endurance and encouragement

Joshua 1

*'... do not be discouraged, for the L*ORD *your God will be with you wherever you go.' (v.9)*

What promises and words of encouragement has God spoken to you? Can you hold on to those as you enter times of hardship, suffering or darkness? Do you need to take courage in a way that perhaps you have never known before? My experience is that the only way to come out of the valley of the shadow of death a stronger person is to go in holding on to God's promises and draw on them in times of darkness.

8 November

Forgiving parents

Luke 2:41–52

*'Your father and I have been anxiously
searching for you.' (v.48)*

M ary and Joseph must have been frantic as
they returned to Jerusalem to search for
Jesus. However, the beautiful theme of this
account is not the brilliance of the young Jesus but
the loving forgiveness shown by Joseph and Mary.
In this loving and forgiving atmosphere, Jesus was
enabled to grow spiritually. May we also forgive
without blame, nurture without criticism and create a
loving, forgiving home.

24 February

Seeking the Lord

Psalm 34:4–10

'I sought the LORD, and he answered me; he delivered me from all my fears. Those who look to him are radiant; their faces are never covered with shame. This poor man called, and the LORD heard him; he saved him out of all his troubles. The angel of the LORD encamps around those who fear him, and he delivers them. Taste and see that the LORD is good; blessed is the man who takes refuge in him. Fear the LORD, you his saints, for those who fear him lack nothing. The lions may grow weak and hungry, but those who seek the LORD lack no good thing.'

7 November

Forgiving the enemy

Matthew 5:43–48

'But I tell you: Love your enemies ...' (v.44)

In his book, *Strength to Love*, Dr Martin Luther King wrote: 'We never get rid of an enemy by meeting hate with hate; we get rid of an enemy by getting rid of enmity.' These inspired words came from his belief in the eventual triumph of love over hatred. The words of Jesus to forgive and love our enemies go against all our natural inclinations, but then, look where natural inclinations have got us!

25 February

We all need a refuge!

Psalm 34

'Taste and see that the LORD is good; blessed is the man who takes refuge in him.' (v.8)

The Hebrew word for 'refuge' is *châçâh*, which means to flee for protection, to confide in and to hope in someone. It is often used figuratively, in putting trust in God and God being our stronghold. In what ways is God your mighty fortress? However strong we are, we all need a refuge. I am reminded of Elijah seeking refuge from Jezebel. Is your refuge a hiding-place or is it somewhere you meet with God?

6 November

Forgiving a nation

Jeremiah 31:31–34

'For I will forgive their wickedness and will remember their sins no more.' (v.34)

Jeremiah wrote, for the most part, messages laden with doom for a nation which deliberately disobeyed God's commands. Amazingly, in the midst of all his warnings, Jeremiah is inspired to reveal the heart of the living God. A personal, loving, forgiving God, who not only longs for His people to repent, but promises to forget their sins altogether! This is a stupendous revelation of saving grace.

26 February

Compassion and companionship

Lamentations 3:19–26

'… for his compassions never fail. They are new every morning …' (vv.22–23)

God loves us whether we feel it or not. Until a certain stage in their development, babies lack the ability to hold on to the positive experiences of their principal caregivers if the caregiver is not there in person. It is an important milestone when babies acquire the ability to experience love in the absence of the one who loves them. Have you reached that milestone spiritually?

5 November

Ultimate forgiveness

Luke 23:32–43

'Jesus said, "Father, forgive them, for they do not know what they are doing."' (v.34)

I don't believe I have come across one person who has not, at some point in his or her life, received a deep emotional, physical or spiritual wound. Some people seem to have been all but destroyed by bitterness and revenge, while others have turned their lives around by choosing the path of forgiveness. Remind yourself that Jesus, even in His agony, breathes 'Father, forgive them.'

27 February

Meeting on the mountain

Exodus 34:1–10,29

'Present yourself to me there on top of the mountain.' (v.2)

God requested that Moses present himself at the top of Mount Sinai and Moses' obedience resulted in God descending in the cloud. Moses' time on Mount Sinai envisioned, prepared and equipped him for what God was calling him to do. Mountains are places where visions are released. If we want to be sustained in the valleys we must be prepared to scale the heights and meet God in holy places.

4 November

The freedom of forgiveness

Luke 13: 10– 17

'When Jesus saw her, he called her forward and said to her, "Woman, you are set free from your infirmity."' (v.12)

Whatever evil power had imprisoned the woman for eighteen years was instantly broken by the touch of Jesus' hands. Jesus gave her back her life. Is something crippling your heart and mind? Fear of a violent partner? Shame of past abuse? Feel Jesus stretching out His hand to touch you right now – accept His forgiveness – then pass His forgiveness to those who have hurt you. Stand tall – get back your life.

28 February

Preparing to climb

Exodus 33:12–23

'My Presence will go with you, and I will give you rest.' (v.14)

One of the well-known mountain climbers in the Bible is Moses. If we want to meet God in a holy place, at the top of a mountain, we need to be teachable and to desire to follow His ways. Moses didn't simply ask to remain in God's favour, he recognised the importance of really knowing God and of living according to His ways. How well do you know God? We need to read our Bibles to know Him and His character.

3 November

Straight and praising God

Luke 13: 13, 15– 16

'Then he put his hands on her, and immediately she straightened up and praised God ... The Lord answered [the synagogue ruler], "You hypocrites! Doesn't each of you on the Sabbath untie his ox or donkey from the stall and lead it out to give it water? Then should not this woman, a daughter of Abraham, whom Satan has kept bound for eighteen long years, be set free on the Sabbath day from what bound her?"'

29 February

Friendship and filling

Psalm 16

'... *you will fill me with joy in your presence* ...' *(v.11)*

Life consists of both joyful mountaintop and sad valley experiences. Our spiritual mountaintop encounters with God bring with them bedrock of belief and personal experience of the friendship of God. It is on the mountain that we are filled, spiritually and emotionally, and have a reserve on which to draw when in the valley. What are your mountaintop experiences? How have you been impacted by them?

2 November

A living sacrifice

Psalm 94

'The LORD will not abandon his people; he will not desert those who belong to him.' (v.14, GNB)

Psalm 94 shows us a God who gave us our ears and hears our cries; who made our eyes and sees our troubles. The psalmist knows what it feels like to be anxious, to be near to death, to be persecuted (vv.16–19). But he also has experience of God as a comforter and refuge. He has been protected and defended by a God who cares. God did not abandon him in his hour of need, and He will not abandon us.

1 March

Treasures in the darkness

Isaiah 45:2–22

'I will give you the treasures of darkness, riches stored in secret places …' (v.3)

A hyacinth bulb needs to be left in the dark in order to produce the colourful and highly fragrant flower for which it is renowned. I wonder what your darkness is? Is it physical pain, past hurt; difficult circumstances, spiritual doubt or dryness? These moments have the potential to bear the beautiful fruit; but we do not always see the result until the darkness has passed and we are in the light.

1 November

Holding on

Judges 6:1–16

'"But sir," Gideon replied, "if the LORD is with us, why has all this happened to us? ..."' (v.13)

God does not abandon us. But sometimes if we feel He has and we can make no sense of our situation, what can we do? Hold on – and like Gideon keep the channels of communication open, even if we feel we do not get an answer. We can ask God why all this has happened to us and we can ask others to pray when we cannot. When we are too exhausted to pray, we can let God and others help us to carry the burden.

2 March

A blessing

Numbers 6:22–27

'The LORD said to Moses, "Tell Aaron and his sons, 'This is how you are to bless the Israelites. Say to them: '"The LORD bless you and keep you; the LORD make his face shine upon you and be gracious to you; the LORD turn his face towards you and give you peace."' So they will put my name on the Israelites, and I will bless them."'

31 October

Offer yourselves

Romans 12:1–2

'Offer yourselves as a living sacrifice to God, dedicated to his service and pleasing to him.' (v.1, GNB)

When things go wrong we look for reasons and answers. Was it our fault, or someone else's? If we offer ourselves as a living sacrifice, we are pleasing to God. So the surprising answer is that we can reveal God's power and glory through offering ourselves to Him. It is not what happens to us that is important, but our reaction to it. God can use the difficult times in our lives to reveal His glory.

3 March

God bless you

Ephesians 5:8–20

'Speak to one another with psalms, hymns and spiritual songs.' (v.19)

So what's the best thing we can communicate to one another? Surely it is the blessing of the Lord. Paul tells us to speak to one another with 'psalms, hymns and spiritual songs'. We may feel a little embarrassed about doing that, but prayerfully blessing one another with our words, actions, touch and gesture communicates God's love. After all – that's what we're here for.

30 October

God's mercy

Ephesians 2:1–10

'God, who is rich in mercy, made us alive with Christ even when we were dead in transgressions …' (vv.4–5a)

How is Paul (in Romans 12), able to ask his readers to present themselves as living sacrifices? The answer, he says, is because of God's great mercy. Paul says that we have all gone our own way, and followed our own desires rather than God's. But the God we rebel against, and who has us at His mercy, shows us mercy, by sending Jesus and restoring the relationship we have broken.

4 March

Whole life communication

2 Corinthians 5: 11 – 15

'For Christ's love compels us …' (v.14)

I t was said of the ballerina, Dame Margot Fonteyn, that her every move and gesture spoke about her life in ballet. Dancing was a compulsion. Very little that she did escaped its influence. 'Christ's love compels us,' says Paul. We should be moved by His love. Urged on to share it. The dance of life that celebrates our salvation should be so beautiful that others want to learn it too.

29 October

A chosen people

Ephesians 1:3–14

'For he chose us in him before the creation of the world to be holy and blameless in his sight.' (v.4)

God has revealed the mystery at the heart of the universe, which is that all things come together in Jesus. In Him the universe finds its meaning. Jesus is its source, sustainer and goal. God has chosen us in His plan and, says Paul, has sealed us with the Holy Spirit, like a deposit guaranteeing our full inheritance. It is in the light of all this, that Paul appeals to us to be living sacrifices.

Careless talk costs lives

Ephesians 4:17–32

'Do not let any unwholesome talk come out of your mouths …' (v.29)

There was a wartime saying that 'careless talk costs lives'. It's a warning we would still do well to heed as careless talk costs the lives of our fellowships dearly. If we are truly seeking to live as God's children our speech is not something we just have to keep an eye – or an ear – on, it's part of a whole package which governs the way we communicate with one another in every sense.

28 October

Reasons to be cheerful

Genesis 1

'God saw all that he had made, and it was very good ...' (v.31)

God created our world and delighted in it. He decided that fish would swim in the sea, and stars would shine in the sky. When He had finished He looked round at all that He had made, and decided that it was very good. There was trouble ahead, but nonetheless God was pleased with His creation. Today let's take nothing for granted, but rejoice in God's handiwork.

6 March

Seasoned conversation

Colossians 4:2–6

'Let your conversation be always full of grace …' (v.6)

Imagine that a poor conversation is like a casserole without seasoning, palatable but bland. Seasoning not only brings out the taste, it preserves something good within us. The recipe for good conversation is as much about what we leave *out* of the ingredients as what we put in. One wrong flavour can mess up the taste and swamp what's best. The balance is up to us. Ask God to keep your conversation seasoned!

27 October

Created in His image

Genesis 1:27–28

'So God created man in his own image, in the image of God he created him; male and female he created them. God blessed them and said to them, "Be fruitful and increase in number; fill the earth and subdue it. Rule over the fish of the sea and the birds of the air and over every living creature that moves on the ground."'

7 March

Intimacy with God

Psalm 139

'O Lᴏʀᴅ, you have searched me and you know me.' (v.1)

Despite our faults, God still loves us, but there is a difference between intimacy and familiarity. David retains the sense of awe and wonder that our relationship with God must contain. Lose the awe and wonder and we lose the sense of the magnitude of God's call on our life and His intervention in it. Intimacy begins with being face to face. His face is turned towards yours – will you turn to meet His gaze?

26 October

A willing offering

Romans 6: 11–23

' … but rather offer yourselves to God, as those who have been brought from death to life.' (v.13)

Paul says that because of God's mercy we should offer ourselves to God as a living sacrifice. Our response is to choose whether we offer ourselves or not. If we offer ourselves to God it must be done willingly. We should not be reluctant living sacrifices. Neither should we be like a little child and snatch back what we have offered when it suits us.

8 March

Honest to God

Psalm 22:1–19

'My God, my God, why have you forsaken me?' (v.1)

God hates hypocrisy. God loves an honest and searching heart. And if that heart is torn with grief and burdened with doubt – then we're *really* talking! For even if our heart is honestly turned to Him in the appeal of 'why?' He can reach it with His comfort, and it won't be long before He melts it with His love and leads us through to a more trusting place. So, when you pray – be honest.

25 October

Living for God

Psalm 119:9–16

'How can a young man keep his way pure? By living according to your word.' (v.9)

We do not offer our sacrifice in the Temple, but in our daily lives. Here the psalmist shows how we can go about it. We need to live according to God's Word and be ever watchful and devoted to God (v.10). We need to commit God's Word to memory (v.11). We need to get our understanding from God (v.12) and share the truth we discover (v.13). Finally we need to meditate on what God reveals to us (v.15).

9 March

Written on our hearts

Deuteronomy 6:4–9

'Hear, O Israel: The LORD our God, the LORD is one. Love the LORD your God with all your heart and with all your soul and with all your strength. These commandments that I give you today are to be upon your hearts. Impress them on your children. Talk about them when you sit at home and when you walk along the road, when you lie down and when you get up. Tie them as symbols on your hands and bind them on your foreheads. Write them on the door-frames of your houses and on your gates.'

24 October

Surrendering our rights

Philippians 2:1–18

'And being found in appearance as a man, he humbled himself …' (v.8)

J esus was 'in very nature God', but instead of demanding His rights, He let them go, became human and humbled Himself, to the point of dying on the cross. As living sacrifices Paul says that if we are now united in Christ, then instead of insisting on our rights and being selfish, we should be humble and consider others' interests as important as ours.

Glorious graffiti

Deuteronomy 6:4–9

'Write them on the door-frames of your houses and on your gates.' (v.9)

One of the greatest challenges we face is in communicating a love for God, His law and His Word in a way that isn't negative and stuffy. Even if we indulge in a bit of glorious graffiti! The current trend in sweatshirts and caps with a message may not be to our taste, but it gets the idea. Consider how you might follow these guidelines in a contemporary sense – without being cringeworthy!

23 October

Giving up and laying down

Matthew 19:16–30

'Peter answered him, "We have left everything to follow you! What then will there be for us?"' (v.27)

Sacrificing always hurts whether its giving up chocolate or saving money. The disciples left behind homes, families and jobs to follow Jesus. We should count the cost of following Him. It may cost us in terms of time, relationships, money and effort. But we also need to hear from God what He will give us. Let's spend some time listening to Him. What is He calling us to give up or lay down?

11 March

A solitary place

Mark 1:35–39

'Very early in the morning … Jesus got up … and went off to a solitary place, where he prayed.' (v.35)

Prayer was the very essence of Jesus' relationship with His Father. He prayed regularly, honestly, and often in a quiet, solitary place very early in the morning, before the pressures and demands of the day took His attention. If Jesus needed to begin His day this way – how much more do we! Ask God to find you a quiet and solitary place to spend time with Him today – and look out for the unexpected!

22 October

Trusting God

Hebrews 11

'Now faith is being sure of what we hope for and certain of what we do not see.' (v.1)

As living sacrifices we need to trust God. Hebrews tells us that the 'ancients' had faith and were praised for it. But if we read the full stories of those mentioned, Abraham, Moses and David, we find they certainly got things wrong. They made mistakes. They got angry with God. They despaired. But above all else, they loved God, listened to Him and tried their best to understand and follow Him.

12 March

No words necessary

Romans 8:18–27

*'… but the Spirit himself intercedes for us
with groans that words cannot express.' (v.26)*

Sometimes, words fail us in prayer. We may not
even be sure *what* we should pray; or it could be
that our heart is breaking. The situation we face,
or face on behalf of another, is too painful or complex
to put into words. That is when, Paul says, '… the Spirit
helps us in our weakness' (v.26). Sometimes we need
few words, and even when we have none, 'the Spirit
himself intercedes for us'.

21 October

More reasons to be cheerful

John 17

'And now, Father, glorify me in your presence with the glory I had with you before the world began.' (v.5)

God chose to enter our world; to become part of His creation through the Person of Jesus. He opened Himself up to all the vulnerability, pain and humiliation that this world offers; and He died. At the heart of the universe is love, but God's love is not a weak despairing love, it is a powerful transforming love. It ends not with the cross, but leads into resurrection, so that we may have eternal life.

13 March

Taming the tongue

James 3:1–12

'Likewise the tongue is a small part of the body, but it makes great boasts …' (v.5)

These verses contain vivid metaphorical warnings from James. For the damage our 'fiery' words can do may be irreversible and far-reaching. Scalding, charring and laying waste – our tongue needs taming. But we cannot do this alone. We need the help of the Holy Spirit, a life soaked in prayer and God's Word; and, if we are brave, someone to whom we can be accountable.

This is eternal life

John 17:1–4

'After Jesus said this, he looked towards heaven and prayed: "Father, the time has come. Glorify your Son, that your Son may glorify you. For you granted him authority over all people that he might give eternal life to all those you have given him. Now this is eternal life: that they may know you, the only true God, and Jesus Christ, whom you have sent. I have brought you glory on earth by completing the work you gave me to do."'

Slow to speak, quick to listen

James 1:19–27

'Everyone should be quick to listen, slow to speak and slow to become angry …' (v.19)

Listening involves more than just hearing the sounds and sentiment of the words of others. We need to listen with our eyes, with the benefit of experience, and with genuine empathy that turns us around to stand in the place of the one who is speaking. Those are tough requirements in a busy day, but genuine listeners give a gift of a space and a measure of dignity to the one being listened to.

19 October

Promises, promises

1 Kings 8:56–61

'But your hearts must be fully committed to the LORD our God.' (v.61)

Solomon places the ark of the covenant, the symbol of the promises made by God and Israel, into the newly-built Temple. Then he praises God and reminds the Israelites how faithful and committed God has been to them. 'Not one word has failed,' Solomon says. God has kept His promises to His people. He can be trusted. As living sacrifices we are also called to keep our promises to God.

'Greetings!'

Luke 1:39–45

'As soon as the sound of your greeting reached my ears, the baby in my womb leaped for joy.' (v.44)

I often wonder what Mary called out in her greeting to her cousin Elizabeth. In our rushed and too-much-to-do world we have lost something of the art of genuine greeting on meeting, phoning or writing to one another. Greetings are worth some thought and effort – they literally are our 'first word' in communication. Who will you greet today and how can you do so with genuine joy and welcome?

18 October

Here I am

1 Samuel 3:1–21

'Then Samuel said, "Speak, for your servant is listening."' (v.10b)

In Romans 12 Paul tells us that as living sacrifices we should be dedicated to God's service. Samuel was dedicated to God by his mother, Hannah, who made a promise to God that if He gave her a child, that child would be His. If we are to be dedicated to God, we cannot rely on vows or actions taken on our behalf. Like Samuel, we have to choose, ourselves, to listen to God and act on what He tells us.

16 March

He knows us

John 10: 11 – 12,14 – 16

'I am the good shepherd. The good shepherd lays down his life for the sheep. The hired hand is not the shepherd who owns the sheep. So when he sees the wolf coming, he abandons the sheep and runs away. Then the wolf attacks the flock and scatters it … I am the good shepherd; I know my sheep and my sheep know me – just as the Father knows me and I know the Father – and I lay down my life for the sheep. I have other sheep that are not of this sheep pen. I must bring them also. They too will listen to my voice, and there shall be one flock and one shepherd.'

17 October

Serving God

1 Corinthians 12

'There are different kinds of service, but the same Lord.' (v.5)

The services we perform for God will vary according to our age and circumstances. Paul says that the important thing is that all our gifts and abilities are given by the Holy Spirit for the common good. Those who make tea after worship and befriend the newcomers, are performing a service to the same Lord as those with other gifts and abilities. Take the time to review your own service to God. Are you doing too much or too little?

17 March

Following the Shepherd's voice

John 10:24–30

'My sheep listen to my voice; I know them, and they follow me.' (v.27)

We need to look at some of the practicalities of following Jesus' example and consider how we should apply some wider biblical teaching on communication. But, as ever, we first need to begin at the feet of the Shepherd. As Christians, it is His voice that we should follow more than any other. He knows us well and as we get to know Him better we will increasingly distinguish the sound of His voice and learn to follow.

16 October

Pleasing God

Matthew 3:13–17

'And a voice from heaven said, "This is my Son, whom I love; with him I am well pleased."' (v.17)

Jesus had not begun His ministry, He had been leading an ordinary life as a carpenter's son, so why was God pleased with Him? We do not know the full answer, but part of it must be that Jesus was obedient to His Father, and always wanted to do His will. In our ordinary lives, day by day, our obedience to God will please Him. God says to us, 'You are My child, whom I love, with you I am well pleased.'

18 March

Spoken in silence

Matthew 27:11–14

'But Jesus made no reply …' (v.14)

Silence can imply consent. There are times when we must speak out rather than allow injustice, cruelty, slander or lies to remain unchallenged. But Jesus' example here is to speak only when words are needed, and to know the power of silence in the face of accusation. Silence also gives God a chance to speak into a situation and gives us a quiet moment to pray before speaking more carefully considered words.

15 October

A broken heart

Psalm 51

'The sacrifices of God are a broken spirit …' (v.17)

In Romans 12:1 Paul calls us to offer true worship to God. This true worship is about the state of our relationship with Him. If you are trying to hide something from God, then you, like the psalmist, can replace the misery of sin with the joy of a new relationship with God. You can start afresh by genuinely saying sorry, because, 'a broken and contrite heart, O God, you will not despise'.

19 March

Tears of compassion

John 11:32–43

'Jesus wept.' (v.35)

Jesus never remained unmoved by the pain of others. Through the cross, our pain became His pain too and communicated His love and compassion. We may rarely have the answers to others' pain, but we can simply 'be'. Be with them in their grief, be alongside them in their pain or, like Jesus, be prepared to share their tears. In doing so we are hearing their pain. That's a very special kind of communication.

14 October

Even more reasons to be cheerful

John 16:5–16

'It is for your good that I am going away. Unless I go away, the Counsellor will not come to you; but if I go, I will send him to you.' (v.7)

The presence of the Holy Spirit showed the believers that they had been born again, and that God loved them (Rom. 5:5). The Holy Spirit brought blessing, fellowship, freedom, peace and wisdom. His work is ongoing. He is still helping us as believers. The Holy Spirit still brings joy to God's people. Take time to thank God that He does not leave us comfortless, and ask Him for an awareness of His presence.

20 March

An extravagant gesture

Matthew 26:6–13

'Aware of this, Jesus said to them, "Why are you bothering this woman? She has done a beautiful thing to me." ' (v.10)

Jesus says that the actions of this ordinary woman will be known throughout the world wherever the gospel is preached. That special comment assures me that Jesus loves it when we are extravagant towards Him, and one another, in love and gratitude. Not necessarily materially extravagant, but extravagant in terms of time, effort, gifts and creativity. Extravagant gestures communicate extravagant love.

13 October

The Spirit of truth

John 16: 12–15

'I have much more to say to you, more than you can now bear. But when he, the Spirit of truth, comes, he will guide you into all truth. He will not speak on his own; he will speak only what he hears, and he will tell you what is yet to come. He will bring glory to me by taking from what is mine and making it known to you. All that belongs to the Father is mine. That is why I said the Spirit will take from what is mine and make it known to you.'

21 March

He spoke with relevance

Matthew 13:3– 13,34–35

'Then he told them many things in parables, saying …' (v.3)

Jesus knew how to captivate a crowd and leave them with images and connections which would enable them to carry His message away with them. Parables enabled His presentation of God's kingdom to draw parallels with day-to-day living and to be relevant. How often do we share God's story – in the pulpit or the pub – with such cultural and personal relevance that people really listen?

12 October

A different perspective

Psalm 73

'… till I entered the sanctuary of God; then I understood their final destiny.' (v.17)

Are you discouraged and dismayed because all around you evil seems to prosper? The psalmist struggled to understand until, he says, 'I entered the sanctuary of God'. He realises that this life is like a dream, and when the perspective changes, and he looks at things through God's eyes, he sees the true reality. This world is not the end; God sees things through the perspective of eternity.

22 March

He spoke with
authority

Matthew 4:19–20

' "*Come, follow me,*" *Jesus said … At once they
left their nets and followed him.*' (vv.19–20)

Authority depends on experience and confidence in the one who speaks, and respect and trust from those who listen. It must also have a clear and recognised source. Jesus' authority always gives a call to discipleship which is clear and uncompromising. There are no ifs, buts or maybes. No wavering or wasting of words. He simply says 'Do this and I will do that.' Jesus called, they followed.

11 October

Here today, gone tomorrow

Luke 12:13–21

'You have plenty of good things laid up for many years. Take life easy; eat, drink and be merry.' (v.19)

I f we look from God's perspective our views begin to change. Jesus showed the rich man how little control he had over his life; and challenged him about what would happen to him and to his wealth when he died. We need to ask ourselves whether we view success by the standards of this world. Do we make choices in our lives based on how others will view us? We should not conform to the standards of this world.

23 March

Speaking or listening?

'Jesus … was transfigured before them. His clothes became dazzling white, whiter than anyone in the world could bleach them. And there appeared before them Elijah and Moses, who were talking with Jesus. Peter said to Jesus, "Rabbi, it is good for us to be here. Let us put up three shelters – one for you, one for Moses and one for Elijah." (He did not know what to say, they were so frightened.) Then a cloud appeared and enveloped them, and a voice came from the cloud: "This is my Son, whom I love. Listen to him!"'

10 October

God wants failures

1 Corinthians 1:18–31

'For the foolishness of God is wiser than man's wisdom …' (v.25)

We are told that God deliberately chooses the weak, the foolish and the lowly to do His work. Do you feel a failure? Do you regard others as failures? A change of perspective may give you a different view. It may be that your apparent failure will be used to bring about God's glory. Do you feel weak, foolish or lowly? Then you are just the kind of person that God is looking for to fulfil His work.

24 March

Listen to Him!

Mark 9:1–7

'This is my Son, whom I love. Listen to him!' (Mark 9:7)

God's gift of His Son was His ultimate communication with us. So when that Son began His earthly ministry, it was obvious that He should have something to say worth listening to! Peter often needed things spelled out. (He gives me so much hope!) I think that exclamation mark at the end of the verse is vital for 'spelling out' the importance of listening to Jesus! How well do you listen to Him?

9 October

Dare to be different

2 Samuel 6: 12–23

'And when she saw King David leaping and dancing before the LORD, she despised him in her heart.' (v.16)

King David was so excited that the ark of the covenant was entering Jerusalem, that 'he danced before the LORD with all his might'. His wife, Saul's daughter, saw him, misunderstood and despised him. In our response to God we may not conform to the norm. It may be in our work, family or even church that as Christians we cannot follow an accepted practice, but dare to be different to please God.

25 March

God speaks through our conscience

John 8:1–11

'At this, those who heard began to go away one at a time …' (v.9)

Paul says that the requirements of God's law are written on our hearts so that our consciences can bear witness to that law and accuse and defend our thoughts and actions accordingly (Rom. 2:14–15). We do need to be cautious, however, for it is possible for our consciences to deceive us. Jesus challenges the crowd by relying on their response to what their consciences are saying to them.

Be transformed

Acts 9:1–22

'All those who heard him were astonished and asked,
"Isn't he the man who caused havoc …?"' (v.21a)

Take time today to listen to God. Is there some part of your life that He wishes to transform? Is there a burden you need to let go? Are strong negative emotions keeping you imprisoned? The same transforming power that stopped Paul in his tracks, and dropped him to his knees, is available to us today. Nothing is too hard for God. Give Him your problems and let Him transform them, and you.

26 March

God speaks through relationships

1 John 4:7–21

'… let us love one another, for love comes from God. Everyone who loves has been born of God …' (v.7)

In this beautiful passage Paul gives us the rhyme and reason for Christian love. God first loved us sacrificially through the gift of His Son, therefore we should love one another. It is in the sharing of that love that God speaks, whether it is love between Christians or even between unbelievers. *The Thematic Bible* says that 'Human love is enobled by being patterned on God's love for his people'.

7 October

Still more reasons to be cheerful

Revelation 21:1–7

'He will wipe every tear from their eyes. There will be no more death or mourning or crying or pain, for the old order of things has passed away.' (v.4)

We have a creative Father who saw that His creation was good; we have the loving Son who redeems us; we have a powerful Spirit that guides us; and we have a destiny awaiting us. God is the beginning and the end, and our end is eternal relationship with God. A future without sadness or pain or fear. God knows our sufferings and our reward awaits us in eternity.

27 March

God speaks through His creation

Romans 1:18–25

'For since the creation of the world God's invisible qualities … have been clearly seen …' (v.20)

It's true that sometimes we don't see what we're looking for even when it is staring us in the face. Perhaps that's why my husband frequently asks, 'Where's the …?' while gazing into the depths of the cupboard. I then appear alongside to point out the 'invisible' object which is usually right in front of his nose! Creation is God's love letter to us that is right in front of our nose!

6 October

A beautiful bride

Revelation 21:1–3

'Then I saw a new heaven and a new earth, for the first heaven and the first earth had passed away, and there was no longer any sea. I saw the Holy City, the new Jerusalem, coming down out of heaven from God, prepared as a bride beautifully dressed for her husband. And I heard a loud voice from the throne saying, "Now the dwelling of God is with men, and he will live with them. They will be his people, and God himself will be with them and be their God."'

28 March

God speaks through the Bible

Psalm 119:89–105

'Your word is a lamp to my feet and a light for my path.' (v.105)

The Bible is our practical handbook for Christian living as well as a source of inspiration, comfort and care. God's Word could make the way so much clearer for us yet often we keep it for emergencies. We forget that if we would only use it regularly to illuminate our path on every occasion we might just avoid those everyday cuts and bruises and really discover the power of the guiding Word of God.

5 October

Changing our minds

Colossians 3:1–14

'*Set your minds on things above, not on earthly things.*' (v.2)

As living sacrifices we are to be transformed inwardly by a complete change of our minds (Rom. 12:2). The transformation which is begun when we believe in Christ, and which continues all our lives, brings new responsibilities and challenges. Our minds should have a complete reorientation, rather than occasionally having a holy thought. Today is a good day for a spiritual spring clean.

29 March

God speaks through Jesus

John 1:1–5

'In the beginning was the Word, and the Word was with God, and the Word was God.' (v.1)

Jesus is the Word of God incarnate who makes God's love known through His words and deeds, His life and, more specifically, His death. His was a life and death which communicated just how much God loves us. God gave His Son as the ultimate sacrifice making us right with Him. That's true communication. Jesus is God's ultimate Word of love for us. How should that influence the way we share Him with others?

4 October

Knowing God's will

Acts 22:1–21

'Then he said, "The God of our fathers has chosen you to know his will."' (v.14)

We should be open to God using all manner of messengers to show us His will. Do you know God's will for you? Maybe someone has been suggesting you do something, and you haven't recognised it as God speaking to you through someone else. Paul was given his assignment by another believer. If you already know God's will for you but are hesitating as Ananias did, listen for God's reassurance, and then 'go'.

30 March

Love is...

1 Corinthians 13:2–8

'If I have the gift of prophecy and can fathom all mysteries and all knowledge, and if I have a faith that can move mountains, but have not love, I am nothing. If I give all I possess to the poor and surrender my body to the flames, but have not love, I gain nothing. Love is patient, love is kind. It does not envy, it does not boast, it is not proud. It is not rude, it is not self-seeking, it is not easily angered, it keeps no record of wrongs. Love does not delight in evil but rejoices with the truth. It always protects, always trusts, always hopes, always perseveres. Love never fails …'

3 October

Good, pleasing and perfect

John 14:5–14

'I tell you the truth, anyone who has faith in me will do what I have been doing.' (v.12)

Our purpose is to bring glory to God by being living sacrifices. We can ask for anything in Jesus' name, and He will do it, if it brings God glory. And if we live as living sacrifices we will know God's will. We will be like Jesus, as humans were meant to be. Whatever our circumstances we can bring glory to God through a sacrificial life. Let this change our perception of our circumstances.

31 March

Communication – framed by love

1 Corinthians 13:1–7

'If I speak in the tongues of men and of angels, but have not love, I am only a resounding gong or a clanging cymbal.' (v.1)

I have a photo of my son, then aged three, set in a rough red frame. It doesn't fit and the frame is a bit wonky, but because my son made it at nursery and gave it to me for Christmas, it is precious. That wonky frame also frames his love for me. Communication is life and love. The apostle Paul shows us how love should frame our communication. Challenging isn't it?

2 October

A life of joy

Philippians 1:1–6

'I thank my God every time I remember you … I always pray with joy …' (vv.3–4)

Many of us face tough times and the issues confronting us can be so intense and serious that our joy can be eclipsed by all-consuming life difficulties. 'Where is any joy in my life?' we may cry. Paul was persecuted, beaten, stoned, often hungry, and left naked in cold weather. He even wrote this letter of joy in prison. Paul found a joy in living, despite his situation, and so can we.

1 April

Messages matter

Genesis 1:1–11

'And God said, "Let there be light," and there was light.' (v.3)

We have letter, fax, phone and email. We can word message, photo message, text and video conference. But God had the first word, literally. His Word was creative, so creative that He spoke our world into being. Creativity drives true communication. It must do something, change something, give something, make something, as it speaks. God speaks to us because He loves us. Love always seeks to communicate.

1 October

Compassion for friends

Philippians 1:7–11

> *'… I long for all of you with the affection of Christ Jesus.' (v.8)*

One of the reasons for Paul's joy is that his fellow-believers are 'in his heart' and he feels a deep affection for them. Love keeps the way open for God to work in our lives and love produces joy. Paul's love for his fellow-believers is obvious. Is there someone who would appreciate a card or a letter from you today, assuring them of your prayers? Paul's model is worth copying!

God hears

Psalm 28

'... O Lord my Rock; do not turn a deaf ear to me.' (v.1)

Sometimes we behave as if God has selective hearing, that He listens to some people more than others. In fact, God is a great listener. What a relief to find an ear that will never be deaf, a shoulder that will never be turned, a heart that will never be bored! Our God encourages His people to draw near and talk to Him. He is a relational God. Keep talking: He's listening!

30 September

Hit by an 'it'!

James 1:1–18

'Consider it pure joy, my brothers, whenever you face trials of many kinds …' (v.2)

'Oh cheer up, it may never happen', are words that may jar with us. Perhaps our silent response is to scream, 'But, *it* has happened.' 'It' encompasses the struggles we have in the various trials which life throws at us and yet here we read of James encouraging us to 'Consider it pure joy … whenever you face trials of many kinds …' Why? Because 'it' is a way forward to become 'mature and complete'.

3 April

One thing

Psalm 27

'One thing I ask of the Lᴏʀᴅ, this is what I seek …' (v.4)

David's ambition was to simply know the presence of the Lord. Single-hearted devotion is very precious to God. In Luke 10 we read of a woman who was commended by Jesus for the same desire. God saw this devotion in the life of His Son poured out, and declared from heaven, 'This is my beloved, in whom I have great pleasure.' Whenever He sees such devotion it is like a fragrant offering, reminding Him of His Son.

29 September

Not lacking anything

James 1:3–6

'You know that the testing of your faith develops perseverance. Perseverance must finish its work so that you may be mature and complete, not lacking anything. If any of you lacks wisdom, he should ask God, who gives generously to all without finding fault, and it will be given to him. But when he asks, he must believe and not doubt, because he who doubts is like a wave of the sea, blown and tossed by the wind.'

4 April

A clear conscience

Psalm 26

'My feet stand on level ground ...' (v.12)

A clean conscience is priceless. It means we can live without fear or subterfuge, or that sickening sense of guilt, confident that no accusation the enemy could bring against us will stick. The only way to have a clean conscience is to stand at the foot of the cross: to trust in the One who has paid the ultimate sacrifice on our behalf. The price is paid, we are covered. Our feet stand on solid ground.

28 September

Joy of the overcomer

Philippians 1: 12– 18

*'And because of this ... I will continue
to rejoice ...' (v.18)*

When we experience difficult times, see
our dreams shattered and sense that we
are losing control of our lives, what sort of
question do we ask ourselves? We can either ask the
negative, 'Why did this happen to me?' and become
victims. Or we can ask the positive, 'How can I draw
closer to God and how can He be glorified through
this?' and become overcomers. Paul, as we see, did
the latter.

The right way

Psalm 25

'All the ways of the LORD are loving and faithful …' (v.10)

This psalm is a poem about trusting that God's ways are perfect. Sometimes we are tempted to take the easy, selfish way. Obedience seems too hard or costly. But leaving God's highway and pursuing an inviting short cut to personal happiness leads into all sorts of confusion later. We are in this for the long haul, not short-term gratification. Trust Him: stay on course. His 'Well done' is worth waiting for.

27 September

Facing a dilemma

Philippians 1:19–26

'For to me, to live is Christ and to die is gain.' (v.21)

Paul reveals his personal dilemma about life and demonstrates his deep faith in Christ. He is spoilt for choice: which is better, life or death? Dilemmas have the potential to be some of life's joy-stealers. Our only hope of maintaining joy in our decision-making is by making Christ our central focus. If we make it our sole desire to please Jesus, He will help us and guide us through our dilemmas.

Worthy is the Lamb

Revelation 5:10–13

"'You have made them to be a kingdom and priests to serve our God, and they will reign on the earth." Then I looked and heard the voice of many angels … They encircled the throne and the living creatures and the elders. In a loud voice they sang: "Worthy is the Lamb, who was slain, to receive power and wealth and wisdom and strength and honour and glory and praise!" Then I heard every creature in heaven and on earth and under the earth and on the sea, and all that is in them, singing: "To him who sits on the throne and to the Lamb be praise and honour and glory and power, for ever and ever!"'

26 September

Suffering for Christ

Philippians 1:27–30

'Whatever happens, conduct yourselves in a manner worthy of the gospel of Christ.' (v.27)

Paul was trying to teach the Philippians that circumstances are deceiving. At first glance, his suffering and imprisonment seem disastrous for the Church and a terrible waste of his remaining years. That is how it looks, but that is not how it is. Whatever happens … in our own prison of suffering let's faithfully live out the Christian gospel and find the same joy as Paul.

They sang a new song

Revelation 5:6–14

'And they sang a new song: "You are worthy to take the scroll and to open its seals, because you were slain, and with your blood you purchased men for God ..."' (v.9)

Songs come and go; some last a few days, some become 'golden oldies'. It is a source of wonder to me that from a handful of notes can come a perpetual stream of new melodies. It is difficult to encompass this scene from Revelation with human imagination. It is all so overwhelming and glorious. Does God really want to hear my feeble efforts? Of course He does, because the song of the Lamb will be forever new.

25 September

Examine yourself

Philippians 2:1–4

'... then make my joy complete by being like-minded, having the same love ...' (v.2)

Paul challenges the Philippians to take a good look at themselves and how they relate to other Christians. How is it possible to be so unselfish? By becoming so interested in others and in helping them to reach their potential that we forget ourselves in the process. If we let selfishness sneak in like a thief, this can steal our joy and sever relationships. Examine yourself, and bring any selfishness to Jesus.

8 April

The King of glory

Psalm 24

'Who may ascend the hill of the LORD?' (v.3)

Who may stand before Him? Only those who have discovered what God wants: hands that are clean, feet that walk in obedience, a heart cleansed of sinful desires. This prefigured the triumphal entry into glory of One who would ultimately fulfil all the Father's will: would die for the sins of mankind and afterward be received into glory. Let us seek to be godly women, with clean hands and pure hearts.

24 September

Dying to self

Philippians 2:5–11

*'Your attitude should be the same as that
of Christ Jesus.' (v.5)*

'You have an attitude problem', is sometimes
said. According to the dictionary an attitude
is a mental disposition. In today's self-centred
society materialism says: 'Be possessive, please
yourself.' Humanism says: 'Be effective, believe in
yourself.' Pride says, 'Be superior, promote yourself.'
Christ says, 'Be unselfish, humble yourself.' Jesus
'… who for the joy set before him endured the cross'
for others.

The Lord is my Shepherd

Psalm 23

'… he restores my soul.' (v.3)

Simple yet profound, this psalm has steadied, reassured and comforted Christians down the centuries. Just the line, 'The LORD is my shepherd' speaks volumes. It speaks of the intimate care and watchfulness of the shepherd, but also puts in perspective our identity as sheep: vulnerable, limited, trusting. What a tender Shepherd we have! Let His love restore, strengthen and comfort you now.

23 September

Seeing is believing

John 20: 10–18

*'Mary Magdalene went to the disciples with the news:
"I have seen the Lord!"…' (v.18)*

Reflect on the empty cross and the glory of
the resurrection, and like Mary be open to
meeting Jesus in an unexpected way: for He
meets us in our vulnerability and calls each of us, 'My
loved one.' Receive these words into your spirit as
He welcomes you with open arms into His presence.
Rejoice and say, 'I have seen Him.' Then go and tell
someone else that you have met Jesus.

The cross foretold

Psalm 22

'... they have pierced my hands and my feet.' (v.16)

Even in the Old Testament there are many references to the Messiah, and many speak of the crucifixion. This is because the cross is the pivotal point of all God's dealings with humanity. Is the cross central to your life? It is the means of your salvation, the measure of God's amazing love for you. This is where we go to fill our hungry souls; this is where rich and poor kneel on level ground and worship.

22 September

'Why are you crying?'

John 20:14–17

'At this, she turned round and saw Jesus standing there, but she did not realise that it was Jesus. "Woman," he said, "why are you crying? Who is it you are looking for? Thinking he was the gardener, she said, "Sir, if you have carried him away, tell me where you have put him, and I will get him." Jesus said to her, "Mary." She turned towards him and cried out in Aramaic, "Rabboni!" (which means Teacher).'

Before battle and after

Psalms 20 and 21:1–7

'May he give you the desire of your heart …' (20:4);
'You have granted him the desire of his heart.' (21:2)

On the eve of battle David is understandably nervous. But before that, there is work to be done and he knows he needs help! So why was he worried? Experience had taught him that he could not rely on past successes or his reputation. His trust was ultimately in God. The next psalm rejoices in the answer to his prayer: victory in battle! David fought and prayed. Prepare and pre-pray for victory!

21 September

Work it out!

Philippians 2:12–13

'… for it is God who works in you to will and to act according to his good purpose.' (v.13)

The word for 'work out' was the Greek word popularly used for 'working a field'. As a farmer ploughs, sows and weeds before the harvest, so we need to let God 'break up' any hardness of our hearts, sow the seeds of truth, and 'weed out' the things which choke our spiritual lives. Then we shall produce 'good fruit'. God wants to help us fulfil our potential. Thus as we work He is also at work in us!

12 April

Written in the sky!

Psalm 19

'Day after day they pour forth speech …' (v.2)

There are all sorts of ways of speaking; many are not verbal, but visual. What is communicated to you by a flaming sunset, or a majestic mountain? Wonder? Joy? Awe? God wants us to take time to watch and ponder the universe because it is saying something. But the psalm tells us that God also speaks in words. He gives directions for life. Jesus is God's ultimate Word to us. God speaks: are you listening?

20 September

Negativism kills joy

Philippians 2:14–18

'Do everything without complaining or arguing ... shine like stars ...' (vv.14–15)

Grumbling and complaining is a discontented muttering and a negative whining that eats away our inner joy. This attitude of giving voice to negative thoughts can make others feel negative too. Paul challenges us to watch what we say about others and prove that, as Christians, we are different to the world. Our negativism needs to be replaced by a positive attitude that infects the air with joy.

A rejoicing spirit

Luke 1:46–52

'And Mary said: "My soul glorifies the Lord and my spirit rejoices in God my Saviour, for he has been mindful of the humble state of his servant. From now on all generations will call me blessed, for the Mighty One has done great things for me – holy is his name. His mercy extends to those who fear him, from generation to generation. He has performed mighty deeds with his arm; he has scattered those who are proud in their inmost thoughts. He has brought down rulers from their thrones but has lifted up the humble."'

19 September

Friends are important

Philippians 2:19–24

'For everyone looks out for his own interests, not those of Jesus Christ.' (v.21)

It is important to remind ourselves that people are the essential ingredient of life. None of us is a whole, self-sufficient, superwoman. We need one another to complement and enrich our personalities. Paul valued his friendship with Timothy for he had proved himself trustworthy – his character had been tested over time. Friends like Timothy enable us to rejoice. What sort of friend are you?

14 April

Mary's song

Luke 1:35–38,46–56

' "I am the Lord's servant," Mary answered. "May it be to me as you have said." Then the angel left her.' (v.38)

Mary's song was about God and the way He does things, completely contrary to the ways of the world, exalting the lowly and deflating the proud. But she also saw herself in the context of history. From Abraham's seed would come Israel's deliverer. Her plans might have changed, but God's had not! To say, 'I am the Lord's servant', is taking a risk. Are you prepared to have all your plans for the future changed?

18 September

Joy in relationships

Philippians 2:25–30

'Welcome him in the Lord with great joy …' (v.29)

It is often only when we are in need that we find out who our real friends are, but we all need friends like Timothy and Epaphroditus who are there for us when the going gets tough. Friends like this bring a sense of light relief and can make life more bearable. However, the greatest friend we can have is our Saviour, Jesus Christ, who says that our joy may be complete in Him (John 15:11).

What happens when we pray?

Psalm 18:1–19

'… my cry came before him, into his ears.' (v.6)

This psalm has some wonderful lessons in prayer. It begins with a strong confident declaration about God being our rock, strength, shield, refuge. Then the psalmist seems to be hurled into the depths of despair! Does God really care that much? Yes. He crushes the enemy and lifts David out of his trouble and deposits him on safe, solid ground. Keep praying: God always hears and acts on our behalf.

17 September

Driven to prove yourself?

Philippians 3:1–6

'… we who … put no confidence in the flesh …' (v.3)

In today's society we find more and more emphasis put on achievement. Driven people burn themselves out trying to prove themselves. Paul was like that before conversion but his encounter with the risen Jesus Christ revolutionised his life. Hence Paul exhorts the Philippians to 'put no confidence in the flesh' for he has now found his confidence and worth in the free, forgiving love of God.

16 April

The safest place

Psalm 17

'Keep me as the apple of your eye ...' (v.8)

We usually guard our eyes carefully. 'The apple of the eye' is a beautiful metaphor for the sensitive pupil. The psalmist says that just as we guard our eyes from burning sun or swirling dust, so the Lord tenderly protects us. There is also the sense in which the apple of the eye is the object of affection, what a person's eye rests on with the greatest pleasure and delight. We are the apple of God's eye.

16 September

An expression of joy

Psalm 100

'Shout for joy to the Lord, all the earth.' (v.1)

Throughout the Psalms we find an outward expression of exuberant joy portrayed in many different ways: sing for joy (92:4); shout for joy (100:1); clap your hands (47:1); dance and make music to Him with tambourine and harp (149:3); sound the trumpet (150:3). Have you ever explored different ways to offer God an expression of your joy? What about a painting or drawing; poetry or prose?

A compass for life

Psalm 16

'I have set the LORD always before me … I shall not be shaken.' (v.8)

What blessing to see life in terms of growing contentment, security and joy, continuing beyond the grave! Many, if not most, women are discontented with their looks, their marriages, their jobs, their houses. What do many people see ahead of them? Maybe financial struggles and other worries. David set the Lord before him. This is like setting a compass and being confident of our future in God's hands.

15 September

Come before Him

Psalm 100:2–5

'Worship the LORD with gladness; come before him with joyful songs. Know that the LORD is God. It is he who made us, and we are his; we are his people, the sheep of his pasture. Enter his gates with thanksgiving and his courts with praise; give thanks to him and praise his name. For the LORD is good and his love endures for ever; his faithfulness continues through all generations.'

18 April

The fool and the wise man

Psalms 14 and 15

*'He who does these things will never
be shaken.' (15:5)*

Jesus told a parable about a fool who built his house on sand, and a wise person who built on rock. These two psalms similarly contrast two people with totally different outlooks on life. One, shallow and self-important, contemptuously dismisses any appearance of godliness. He lives for now, for the moment. What are you building on? Jesus said it is no good knowing the Word if you don't do it.

14 September

Losses!

Philippians 3:7–11

'… I consider everything a loss compared to the surpassing greatness of knowing Christ Jesus …' (v.8)

What do we regard as achievements? A nice place to go home to, elegant clothes, growing popularity, a great job, the feeling of accomplishment. There is nothing inherently wrong in any of these but they may distract us from what Paul had learnt was the only real source of lasting satisfaction. Paul 'lost all things' for the sake of a new relationship with Jesus Christ. His loss became a gain.

The tyrant's boast

Psalms 10 and 11

'… in all his thoughts there is no room for God.' (10:4)

How do we pray when the fabric of society is undone? These and other psalms show that it is legitimate to call on God to rise up and remove the oppressor. Let us not fall into the same mindset as the oppressor, that in our thinking, 'there is no room for God'. He loves justice and righteousness and uses women like us to make it happen. Pray for cruel regimes to fall; pray 'Thy kingdom come'.

Pressing on ...

Philippians 3: 12–16

'Forgetting what is behind and straining towards what is ahead ...' (v.13)

Paul is clearly a changed man, for his relationship with God now rests on faith and not works. So what now? The Christian life is not passive, it's about progress. Using a picture of a runner, he urges his fellow believers in Philippi to press on in the Christian faith against all opposition and obstacles. He says forget the past and look ahead. Are we aiming to do the same? Let's press on.

20 April

God is my salvation

Isaiah 12:2–6

"Surely God is my salvation; I will trust and not be afraid. The LORD, the LORD, is my strength and my song; he has become my salvation." With joy you will draw water from the wells of salvation. In that day you will say: "Give thanks to the LORD, call on his name; make known among the nations what he has done, and proclaim that his name is exalted. Sing to the LORD, for he has done glorious things; let this be known to all the world. Shout aloud and sing for joy, people of Zion, for great is the Holy One of Israel among you."'

Find some mentors

Philippians 3:17–20

'… take note of those who live according to the pattern …' (v.17)

Paul says to imitate him in our behaviour and our words. However, he also says that we are not to focus fully on one person, no matter how gifted they are. To have a joyful and balanced life we are encouraged to have several mentors. I've been fortunate to follow some wonderfully gifted people and recognise that I've grown as a person as I've integrated their godly lifestyle and wisdom into my own life.

21 April

Water from the well

Isaiah 12

'The LORD … is my strength and my song.' (v.2)

What makes you sing? A spring day? A lovely surprise? If you belong to Him, you have a deep well within you; let down your bucket and draw it up full of truth! Recall to mind His mercies, and let praise surge up through your being, and out of your mouth! Feeling dry? Speak to your soul! 'Come on soul, let's worship God!' The water will begin to flow as you sing and make melody in your heart.

Hold tight

Philippians 4:1

'… my joy … stand firm in the Lord …' (v.1)

I f we are in a boat being tossed around in a squall, we plant our feet slightly apart, grip a rail and use our muscles to keep us standing upright. Similarly, when we are thrown around in the storms of life, we need to stand firm on the promises in Scripture, follow Christ's teaching; tighten our spiritual muscles, and hold on tight to our relationship with our Lord, not letting go of His hand.

22 April

The Creator and creation

Psalm 8

'When I consider your heavens … what is man that you are mindful of him …?' (vv.3–4)

Although David feels so diminished by this immense creation, he is simultaneously struck by the huge significance of mankind. The mighty God who made all this – cattle, birds, fish, as well as stars and moon – really cares about people. Genesis 1:26 tells us we are made in the image of God. He made us in order that we might relate to Him in mutual love and delight, rightly wielding the power He gave us.

10 September

Resolving conflict

Philippians 4:2–3

'I plead with Euodia and … Syntyche to agree with each other in the Lord.' (v.2)

From time to time we experience conflicts with others. How do we handle them? Do we allow these conflicts to grow into unresolved grievances, giving rise to disharmony between us? Or do we recognise that conflicts can be joy-stealers, and therefore choose to work at resolving them? Resolving conflict is not about winning or losing but both sides need to 'agree in the Lord' for harmony to be renewed.

23 April

A cry for justice

Psalms 7 and 9:7–10

'The LORD is a refuge for the oppressed …' (9:9)

I have a friend who was deeply moved by a TV documentary about street children in Mexico. A year later, she was in Guadalajara, enmeshed in the problems of setting up a rescue centre. God expresses His mercy and justice through human agents – women like us. As we pray for justice, let us be open to the possibility that He could move us to become involved in the war of mercy against injustice.

Can I receive?

Romans 5:1–5

'God has poured out his love into our hearts …' (v.5).

Perhaps many of us find it easier to give than receive, and have difficulty in letting others do for us what we so willingly do for them. Most Christians rejoice in telling God that they love Him, but find it hard to accept God's love for *them* personally. But God accepts us totally as we are, and longs that we receive His love; for His love is the security of our hope; and hope brings joy.

24 April

Grief and despair

Psalm 6

'How long, O LORD, how long?' (v.3)

David is totally honest about his emotions. He does not deny them or suppress them, or pretend he is 'fine' when he isn't. He pours out his heart. What is tormenting you? Blighted hopes? Economic collapse? Physical illness? Bereavement? Erring children? Often it is the prolonged nature of the problem which is so hard to bear. God's delays are for our maturing. Our times are in His hands. Don't give up!

8 September

Peace with God

Romans 5:1–4

'Therefore, since we have been justified through faith, we have peace with God through our Lord Jesus Christ, through whom we have gained access by faith into this grace in which we now stand. And we rejoice in the hope of the glory of God. Not only so, but we also rejoice in our sufferings, because we know that suffering produces perseverance; perseverance, character; and character, hope.'

25 April

A morning prayer

Psalm 5

'… make straight your way before me.' (v.8)

David wakes up heavy-hearted, thinking of the day ahead and the problems surrounding him. David's solution was to lay it all out before God and then wait in expectation for Him to show him what to do. Take courage: lay your own case before God, be at peace in your heart as you resolve to take the straight path, not the crooked one. God honours those who seek the straight path.

7 September

Joy – a missing quality?

Philippians 4:4–5

'Rejoice in the Lord always. I will say it again: Rejoice!' (v.4)

Irrespective of how we feel, Paul tells us to, 'Rejoice *in* the Lord *always*.' How can we do that? By reflecting on what the Lord has done for us on the cross, for He is our source of life. His love and goodness give us reason to rejoice. Paul is not encouraging triumphalism or a 'grit your teeth and smile' type of approach, but is saying it is an act of the will to choose to rejoice in God's goodness.

26 April

A good night's sleep

Psalm 4

'Know that the LORD has set apart the godly for himself …' (v.3)

As David determines to trust in God, he finds inward joy returning. Now he can lie down and sleep, knowing that his life is secure. This is the secret of a Christian's happiness. We are surrounded by hurt, frustrated people whose only solution is to live with their anger. We are set apart for God; don't be angry, for what concerns us concerns Him, and He can be trusted to sort things out. Have a good night!

Joy-stealers

Philippians 4:6–7

'Do not be anxious about anything … with thanksgiving, present your requests to God.' (v.6)

Will I cope? Am I adequate? Will it be all right? What if …? These questions we ask ourselves can cause anxiety, and an anxious state of mind can rob us of our sense of joy. Paul urges the Philippians to handle their anxieties by placing the problem squarely in the hands of the One who is in ultimate control. 'In everything, by prayer and petition, with thanksgiving, present your requests to God.'

27 April

A mother in Israel

Judges 5:6–9

'In the days of Shamgar son of Anath, in the days of Jael, the roads were abandoned; travellers took to winding paths. Village life in Israel ceased, ceased until I, Deborah, arose, arose a mother in Israel. When they chose new gods, war came to the city gates, and not a shield or spear was seen among forty thousand in Israel. My heart is with Israel's princes, with the willing volunteers among the people. Praise the LORD!'

A healthy mind

Philippians 4:8–9

'… whatever is true … think about such things.' (v.8)

No matter what we go through, or how bad things seem to be, it is important to deliberatively focus our minds on positive, uplifting thoughts, as this will help us to survive the storms of life. Paul encourages us to think upon 'whatever is true', as opposed to anything false and deceitful. Focusing on good things and God's promises leads to a healthy mind. Meditate on what God says about you.

28 April

The Song of Deborah

Judges 5:1–12

'Wake up, wake up, Deborah! Wake up, wake up, break out in song! Arise, O Barak! Take captive your captives, O son of Abinoam.' (v.12)

Deborah was a woman with a warrior spirit and an ability to hear God. She was not prepared to live perpetually crushed by evil, and when God gave the word she was ready to obey. Her courage instilled faith into Barak. She described herself as a 'mother'. Today, more than ever, we need mothers who are women of courage and conviction, who listen to God, and act in faith and obedience.

4 September

A recipe for happiness

Philippians 4:10–13

'I have learned the secret of being content in any and every situation …' (v.12)

Paul explains that he has 'found the recipe for being happy' (v.12, *The Message*), He reveals that the secret of happiness is not in things, but in a relationship with Jesus Christ. For Paul was convinced that Christ was in the midst of his every day, pouring strength into him to cope with whatever he faced. He learnt a secret: Christ-sufficiency not self-sufficiency gives rise to contentment.

29 April

Doubt and certainty

Psalm 3

'Many are saying …' (v.2)

D avid heard people muttering, 'Many are saying God will not deliver him!' But David had known God too long to doubt. Similarly, you may hear things like: 'No-one believes that any more!' We have an enemy who is a liar and loves to attack our minds with doubt. In Ephesians 6, Paul urges us to put on spiritual armour. We must use the weapons God provides to become strong in the face of doubt and intimidation.

3 September

A generous heart

Philippians 4:14–23

'… my God will meet all your needs according to his glorious riches in Christ Jesus.' (v.19)

Paul talks about the last ingredient for a vibrant and joy-filled Christian life – the quality of generosity. Notice that God meets our needs but not necessarily our wants. They are significantly different. The Philippians were generous to Paul in his need. God is generous to us in our need. How generous are we to others in their need? Let's aspire to be joyful givers with generous hearts.

30 April

The Anointed King

Psalm 2

'The One enthroned in heaven laughs …' (v.4)

At Jesus' baptism a voice declared, 'This is my beloved Son'; and after Pentecost the apostles, quoting this psalm, boldly proclaim that He is also the Anointed King referred to here (Acts 4:25). Be encouraged today! You belong to a King who is gloriously unperturbed by opposition. His long-term plan is slowly but surely unfolding, when all will acknowledge Him. Serve Him; love Him; worship Him.

2 September

Journeying with God

Psalm 139: 1 – 12

'... if I settle on the far side of the sea ... even there your hand will guide me ...' (vv.9 – 10)

'Birth is a beginning, And death a destination ...' So begins a Jewish poem. Life as a journey is a familiar picture. When we become Christians our life journey becomes a spiritual journey too. The route varies – some parts are difficult, some easier. Today's reading reminds us that God is always there for us and ready to put us back on the right track if we stray from the path of righteousness.

1 May

Like a tree

Psalm 1

'… on his law he meditates day and night. He is like a tree planted by streams of water …' (vv.2–3)

When you fly over a desert area it is easy to tell where there is water: a line of green trees stands out against the dusty rock and sand. It should be just as easy to spot someone who loves God's Word and lives according to its principles. Her life will show where the living water is. She nurtures her spirit from the Word of God like a tree drawing water through its roots.

1 September

You are there

Psalm 139:1–3,7–8

'O LORD, you have searched me and you know me. You know when I sit and when I rise; you perceive my thoughts from afar. You discern my going out and my lying down; you are familiar with all my ways … Where can I go from your Spirit? Where can I flee from your presence? If I go up to the heavens, you are there; if I make my bed in the depths, you are there.'

2 May

Beware Babylon!

Isaiah 39

'The time will surely come when everything in your palace … will be carried off to Babylon.' (v.6)

Walking with God is just that. We can't stand still. We can't have a little rest or walk away. We can't choose to go at a faster or slower pace than God. But, even if our erring in the wrong direction brings disastrous consequences, as Hezekiah's did, there is comfort, there is restoration and a new start. Some of the most sublime chapters in the whole Bible are still to come!

31 August

Running away!

Genesis 16:1–15

'Hagar … where have you come from, and where are you going?' (v.8)

The Bible has several examples of God meeting people running away from difficult situations. Here is one of them. Are you running away, literally or metaphorically, from situations or problems you can't face? Do you feel you don't know where you're going but that you can't ask for God's help because you're running away? He loves you! Ask Him to meet with you and give you, like Hagar, a new perspective.

Hezekiah's illness

Isaiah 38

'This is what the Lᴏʀᴅ says: Put your house in order, because you are going to die; you will not recover.' (v.1)

Hezekiah argued with God, stating his own point of view, reminding God how he had walked with Him faithfully. He wept 'bitterly'. And God heard his prayer. Pouring out your heart honestly before God is biblical. It happens all the time in the Psalms, for example. What an amazing insight there is here into a man who walked humbly with his God, yet was prepared to argue with Him.

30 August

Venturing into the unknown

Genesis 24:42–67

'… I prayed, "LORD … please give me success in what I am doing …" ' (v.42, GNB).

Our life's journey may not involve riding off on a camel to marry someone we've never met, but we sometimes need to say 'yes' to God without knowing what that may entail. Realising she was an answer to prayer gave Rebecca the confidence to venture into the unknown. Like her we can trust God with the parts of our journey that are unknown and, like the servant, ask God for success as we trust Him to guide us.

4 May

So that all may know

Isaiah 37: 15– 17,19– 20

'And Hezekiah prayed to the LORD: "O LORD Almighty, God of Israel, enthroned between the cherubim, you alone are God over all the kingdoms of the earth. You have made heaven and earth. Give ear, O LORD, and hear; open your eyes, O LORD, and see; listen to all the words Sennacherib has sent to insult the living God … They have thrown their gods into the fire and destroyed them, for they were not gods but only wood and stone, fashioned by human hands. Now, O LORD our God, deliver us from his hand, so that all kingdoms on earth may know that you alone, O LORD, are God."'

29 August

Stepping out of line?

Numbers 27:1–8

'What Zelophehad's daughters are saying is right … give them property … among their father's relatives …' (v.7)

These sisters had stepped out of line and been rewarded; they had also established a legal precedent for all other women in Israel. Sometimes we may feel we have to 'step out of line' and speak out about something we feel is wrong. It takes courage and faith but if we believe God is prompting us, He will vindicate us. It's better to be 'out of line' and in God's will than 'in line' with injustice.

5 May

Prayer

Isaiah 37:14–20

'Hezekiah received the letter from the messengers and read it. Then he went up to the temple of the LORD and spread it out before the LORD.' (v.14)

How do you pray about things that are troubling you? Hezekiah seeks God's perspective. He lays the problem (the death and suffering of thousands of people) before God and still sees things from God's point of view. He's walked faithfully with God and God hears him. Hezekiah intercedes but he doesn't fight with God. There's plenty to learn from the way Hezekiah lived and prayed.

28 August

Hannah's sacrificial journey

1 Samuel 1: 10–28; 2: 18–21

'… I was pouring out my soul to the LORD.' (1:16)

Sometimes, as we journey with God, like Hannah we may give up something, not necessarily because it's bad, but because it's not helpful or because God wants to see where our priorities lie. But God is overflowingly generous, always giving back to us far more than we have given back or given up for Him. Jesus Himself assures us that anyone who gives up anything for His sake will be amply recompensed (Luke 18:29–30).

6 May

Victory without a fight!

Isaiah 37

'I will put my hook in your nose and my bit in your mouth, and I will make you return by the way you came.' (v.29)

This was an age when each people, each place even, had their own god or gods. And the Assyrians made mincemeat of the gods of all the other peoples they conquered. They were assuming that Judah's Lord, the Almighty God, would be a pushover too. But Hezekiah believed, staked everything, in fact, on the Lord alone being God. May we too follow the Lord in difficult times and see something of His glory.

27 August

A journey in persistence

2 Kings 4:17–37

*'She saddled the donkey and said to her servant,
"Lead on; don't slow down for me unless I tell you."'*
(v.24)

This woman was desperate and went on a journey to Elisha at Carmel, about 25 miles away. She let nothing and no one deter her from reaching the only person she believed could help her in the tragedy confronting her. Her faith and persistence were rewarded. Maybe in our day God is looking for women of persistence in prayer, who will keep going to the Person who can help and not be fobbed off until He acts!

Facing battles

Isaiah 36

*'Has the god of any nation ever delivered his land
from the hand of the king of Assyria?' (v.18)*

What's your experience of spiritual battles?
I once accepted a tight deadline to ghost-
write a book called *God's Heart for the
Poor*, but then I got shingles – lots of pain, no sleep,
no energy. But God took on the battle and I got friends
to pray. But only God's strength, not my weakness,
enabled me to write the book to everyone's
satisfaction. I even sent in the manuscript slightly early!

26 August

Refreshment 'en route'

Psalm 23

'The Lord is my shepherd, I shall not be in want. (v.1)

This psalm reminds us that on our life and spiritual journeys we are not alone. Notice 'lying down' comes before the leading (v.2), and the soul-restoration before the guiding (v.3)! We seem to get it the wrong way round – wearing ourselves to a frazzle before sinking wearily to our knees to ask for help. Perhaps we should get rest and refreshment from the shepherd *before* tackling that long list of 'must do's'.

Highway of Holiness

Isaiah 35:8–10

'… a highway will be there … called the Way of Holiness. The unclean will not journey on it … No lion will be there …' (vv.8–9)

Early Christians were known as 'People of the Way' and it's a good name. As we kneel before Jesus, asking His forgiveness for our unholy ways, He imparts to us His own holiness. He opened up the way to do that through His death on the cross and His resurrection. He redeemed us. He sees us, not as unclean, but clothed in His own white garments of holiness – we've actually become as holy as God is holy!

25 August

My shepherd

Psalm 23

'The LORD is my shepherd, I shall not be in want. He makes me lie down in green pastures, he leads me beside quiet waters, he restores my soul. He guides me in paths of righteousness for his name's sake. Even though I walk through the valley of the shadow of death, I will fear no evil, for you are with me; your rod and your staff, they comfort me. You prepare a table before me in the presence of my enemies. You anoint my head with oil; my cup overflows. Surely goodness and love will follow me all the days of my life, and I will dwell in the house of the LORD for ever.'

9 May

Restoration and transformation

Isaiah 35:1–7

'The desert and the parched land will be glad; the wilderness will rejoice and blossom.' (v.1)

Jesus endured the cross and all its shame for 'the joy set before him' (Heb. 12:2). That joy wasn't going (back) to heaven – which He never *had* to leave in the first place. It was the joy of seeing us restored so we could drink in His life, blossom, be beautiful and fruitful in passing His life on to others. Catch God's joy that we, drinking in His grace, colour the desert with our lives.

24 August

From famine to famine

Ruth 1:1–13

'… Naomi was left without her two sons and her husband.' (v.5)

Naomi had journeyed to Moab in search of 'bread' that could not satisfy (John 6:27). In leaving Bethlehem and the faith of their fathers, the family perhaps demonstrated a lack of faith in God's ability. Their physical hunger was satisfied but they were left spiritually starved. It's sometimes hard in our materialistic society to take as food for the journey 'the bread that God gives' (John 6.33, GNB).

Order and chaos

Isaiah 34

'God will stretch out over Edom the measuring line of chaos and the plumb-line of desolation.' (v.11)

When a house becomes derelict and dangerous sometimes the best policy is to demolish it and rebuild. After His planned and necessary destruction, God 'gathers together', allots and measures out portions then builds something to last forever. Although God's demolition seems hard, when evil reaches a certain pitch, aren't you glad He acts? Otherwise, the world would simply become more evil and chaotic.

23 August

A journey to faith

Ruth 1:6–18

*'But Ruth replied, "… Your people will be my
people and your God my God."' (v.16)*

There are times when we take a huge leap
forward in our spiritual journey and sometimes
this is quite clearly the result of major changes
or events in our physical lives. Often, as in Ruth's case,
these events are not of our choosing and are outside
our control, but God uses them for His own purposes
to 'move us on'. Ask God to use difficult events ahead
to also take you forward spiritually.

11 May

Sins will be forgiven

Isaiah 33:20–22,24

'Look upon Zion, the city of our festivals; your eyes will see Jerusalem, a peaceful abode, a tent that will not be moved; its stakes will never be pulled up, nor any of its ropes broken. There the LORD will be our Mighty One. It will be like a place of broad rivers and streams. No galley with oars will ride them, no mighty ship will sail them. For the LORD is our judge, the LORD is our lawgiver, the LORD is our king; it is he who will save us … No-one living in Zion will say, "I am ill"; and the sins of those who dwell there will be forgiven.'

22 August

A journey in vulnerability

Ruth 1:22–2:22

'So Ruth gleaned in the field until evening. Then she threshed the barley she had gathered …' (2:17)

Ruth's vulnerability as a young widow without male protection, and a 'stranger in the land' allowed God to work! Vulnerability is rarely valued today. Society expects us to put on a confident face, but as we make ourselves vulnerable we learn humility and to trust in God, not in our own abilities. Paul said, 'When I am weak, then I am strong.' Being vulnerable is a valuable step on our spiritual journey.

12 May

Imagining good

Isaiah 32–33

' … till the Spirit is poured upon us from on high, and the desert becomes a fertile field, and the fertile field seems like a forest.' (32:15)

Even though Isaiah was a realist who didn't shy from naming evil for what it was, Heaven was in his heart. Just as it was in Jesus' heart when He saw purity in a demonised prostitute, a faithful follower in a betraying thief, a rock-like witness in an impetuous braggart. What do you see in the people around you? Heaven or hell? It's an important question determining the way you pray for them and treat them.

21 August

A journey in submission

Ruth 3:1–18

'So Ruth went to the threshing place and did just what her mother-in-law had told her.' (v.6, GNB)

Ruth was a remarkable young woman. She did exactly what Naomi told her to do in order to make Boaz aware of his rights and responsibilities under the 'kinsman-redeemer' law. Submitting to someone else, even just at the level of accepting advice, is often a hard step. While we are not to be doormats, submission such as that exemplified here by Ruth is another important stage on our spiritual journey.

13 May

Repentance and rest

Isaiah 30:1–22

'In repentance and rest is your salvation, in quietness and trust is your strength …' (v.15)

The Israelites didn't realise that we have to face God's holiness and repent to find salvation. I've known I've been wrong but, driven by a distorted view of God, I've also failed to see that 'repentance' and 'rest' could co-exist in the same sentence. I've assumed repentance means punishment. I've failed to trust God and believed lies about the One who longs to be gracious and to show us compassion (v.18).

20 August

A journey of joy

Ruth 4

'So Boaz took Ruth home as his wife. The LORD blessed her, and she became pregnant and had a son.' (v.13, GNB)

Ruth the foreigner journeyed from Moab to Bethlehem, from worship of Canaanite gods to worship of the one true God, from barren widowhood to joyful motherhood, but the journey was also one of loyalty, humility, vulnerability and submission. It wasn't easy and she had no idea how God would work things out for her – but she went on in obedience. Ruth's God is our God too – He will work things out as we trust Him.

The Potter and the clay

Isaiah 29:13–24

'You turn things upside down, as if the potter were thought to be like the clay!' (v.16)

Pharisees didn't exist in Isaiah's time, nor do they in ours. But their proud religious spirit does. These people lack God's compassion, humility and vulnerability. They act as if they are the potters and God is the clay, as though God knows nothing and they know everything. It's clay – earth that gets trampled beneath our feet – that the Potter works into amazing vessels for His own use. Imagine that!

19 August

This is your life

Deuteronomy 8:1–10

'Remember how ... God led you ...' (v.2)

Make a 'life map' on a sheet of paper and depict in any way you like your life's events. Start with the fixed points – birth, school, moves, significant events and so on. What your map finally looks like doesn't matter! More important is the process of doing it, remembering and reflecting as you go. As you finish, use the map as a prayer-aid, bringing to God your life journey so far.

Law or grace?

Isaiah 28:9–29

'When a farmer ploughs for planting, does he plough continually … Does he not plant wheat …?' (vv.24–25)

With only 24 hours in a day, we can get so bogged down, so weary with trying to get everything right, that we forget God's good news centres around a love relationship. Frazzled, we try to earn our salvation instead of letting His love and grace transform us. A farmer does not plough every day. If we're yearning for God and walking in His ways then rules and 'ought not to's' become superfluous.

18 August

Living by the Word of God

Deuteronomy 8:1–3

'Be careful to follow every command I am giving you today, so that you may live and increase and may enter and possess the land that the LORD promised on oath to your forefathers. Remember how the LORD your God led you all the way in the desert these forty years, to humble you and to test you in order to know what was in your heart, whether or not you would keep his commands. He humbled you, causing you to hunger and then feeding you with manna … to teach you that man does not live on bread alone but on every word that comes from the mouth of the LORD.'

16 May

City, rock, path and peace

Isaiah 26:1–9

'You will keep in perfect peace him whose mind is steadfast, because he trusts in you.' (v.3)

It can't have been easy for those who had known terrible destruction to remain in perfect peace. Yet that is the context of the famous promise quoted above. After the terrible destruction, God returns things to the way He intended. Imagine living in a city defended by walls and ramparts of salvation, whose gates were always open to the righteous and faithful. I suppose that is what heaven is like.

A Gentile woman's journey

Matthew 15:21–28

'Woman, you have great faith! Your request is granted.' (v.28)

The Gentile woman came to Jesus with her raw pain, her genuine anxiety for her daughter and her audacious faith. Why are we so often less than genuine when we come to God? Are we afraid to be real, afraid He will reject us if we express our anger, our pain, the rawness of our emotions? Now, as in Bible times, God is looking for reality in those who come to Him. And when He finds it, He honours it.

Destruction and salvation

Isaiah 24–25

*'The Sovereign LORD will wipe away the tears …
remove the disgrace of his people …' (25:8)*

I find these chapters hard – the terrifying destruction
and annihilating judgment is terrible. But think of
the whole sweep of the story of salvation history in
the Bible. Time and time again our loving God makes
everything good, but people choose to rebel and
wade ever deeper into selfishness and depravity,
destroying one another until judgment comes and the
God of grace makes all things new again.

16 August

A costly journey

Mark 14:3–9

'She did what she could.' (v.8)

Like others before and since, this unnamed woman was prepared to run the gauntlet of male hostility and criticism in order to express her devotion to Jesus. The part of this woman's story that touches me most deeply is just five words of Jesus: 'She did what she could'. What a commendation! What an epitaph! Which matters more to us – what those around us think, or what our Lord thinks?

A peaceful, rejoicing land

Isaiah 14:4–8

'You will take up this taunt against the king of Babylon: How the oppressor has come to an end! How his fury has ended! The LORD has broken the rod of the wicked, the sceptre of the rulers, which in anger struck down peoples with unceasing blows, and in fury subdued nations with relentless aggression. All the lands are at rest and at peace; they break into singing. Even the pine trees and the cedars of Lebanon exult over you and say, "Now that you have been laid low, no woodsman comes to cut us down."'

15 August

A journey of repentance

Luke 7:36–50

'But he who has been forgiven little loves little.' (v.47)

The woman in this incident was – or had been – a well-known local prostitute. Jesus did not minimise the woman's past, speaking of 'her many sins', but emphasised the forgiveness she had been granted – to the consternation of the other guests. The repentant, forgiven woman is sent away, made whole – like other women who journeyed to Jesus – with the *shalom* wholeness only He can bring to our lives.

19 May

Judgment

Isaiah 14:1–23

'You said in your heart, "I … will raise my throne above the stars of God …" But you are brought down … to the depths of the pit.' (vv.13–15)

Isaiah pronounced against Babylon's ancient king, words we often apply to Satan, 'How you have fallen from heaven, O morning star, son of the dawn!' Remember – when such an arrogant, oppressive, satanic spirit enters into the heart of someone who acquires huge power, God may let him get away with it for a while – but ultimately will bring that person, that regime, down to the pit where it belongs.

14 August

Spiritual progress

John 11:17–43

' … whoever lives and believes in me will never die. Do you believe this?' (v.26)

Previously Jesus had highlighted Martha's wrong priorities (Luke 10:38–42). Now she leaves Mary and the mourners at home to meet Jesus and is rewarded with remarkable insights into Jesus' true nature. Thus it is to Martha, not Mary, that Jesus makes the astounding claim that He is the resurrection and the life, and she responds with a public declaration of her understanding that He is the Messiah and the Son of God.

20 May

My strength and my song

Isaiah 12

'With joy you will draw water from the wells of salvation.' (v.3)

I'm the kind of person who gets stressed and worried pretty easily. Add in some PMT and things can spiral way out of control. I can't seem to get a grip on myself, even though I know God wants me to trust Him. Things only lurch downwards because then I feel totally useless as a Christian, too … unless I remember to do something. Worship bypasses my frenzied brain. If only I remembered to try this sooner!

13 August

A journey to commendation

Mark 12:41–44

'"They all gave out of their wealth; but she, out of her poverty, put in everything …"' (v.44)

A poor widow's journey to give her small offering was commended by Jesus for she generously gave everything she had. He saw not what she gave but what she had left for herself. Some of us don't have much money to spare but we may be less than generous with our time or practical gifts in the service of the kingdom. As Christians we should show generosity of spirit with our time, money and abilities.

21 May

More about the Messiah

Isaiah 11

'... the earth will be full of the knowledge of the LORD as the waters cover the sea.' (v.9)

You could dismiss Isaiah's words as idealistic. Or you could let the worshipping spirit of them seep deep inside you, painting pictures of life in the unfallen world that God made and which He will restore again. His plan has always been for an earth where the youngest child can play in safety and none shall kill or destroy because everyone and everywhere is filled with the knowledge of Him.

12 August

A burden shared

Matthew 11:28–30

'Take my yoke …' (v.29)

Here's another encouraging picture for those who feel tired and burdened on the journey. Yokes enabled two beasts of burden to work together, sharing a load or a task. Jesus offers to share our burdens – those things we must carry with us as we journey and that can weigh us down: perhaps loneliness, caring for a sick relative, failing eyesight or hearing. Jesus says we can be yoked to Him and find rest.

22 May

Christy is coming!

Isaiah 9:1–7

'Of the increase of his government and peace there will be no end.' (v.7)

God breaks the oppressor's might by sending, not an army or thunderbolt, but a Child; gives Him the government and says He will rule in peace, righteousness and justice at last. Remember that He is your Rock. He will be your Wonderful Counsellor, your Mighty God, your Everlasting Father, your Prince of Peace. And His zeal, His vision, His power, not yours, will accomplish everything.

11 August

Come to Jesus

Matthew 11:27–30

'All things have been committed to me by my Father. No-one knows the Son except the Father, and no-one knows the Father except the Son and those to whom the Son chooses to reveal him. Come to me, all you who are weary and burdened, and I will give you rest. Take my yoke upon you and learn from me, for I am gentle and humble in heart, and you will find rest for your souls. For my yoke is easy and my burden is light.'

Fearing God

Isaiah 8

'The LORD Almighty is the one you are to regard as holy, he is the one you are to fear.' (v.13)

What does it mean to 'fear' God? It's not being afraid of Him but it is a paradox. If we 'fear' God – revere Him, hold Him in awe above all others – then He becomes a sanctuary. As we draw closer and rely on Him, we discover that, despite His supreme power, He's loving, not fearful. To those who fear Him – trust Him utterly – He's our rock and hiding place, our foundation which cannot be shaken.

Mary's journey to Elizabeth

Luke 1:39–56

'Blessed is she who has believed that what the Lord has said to her will be accomplished!' (v.45)

Mary 'hurried' to Elizabeth, a journey of about 60 miles. In the Spirit Elizabeth affirmed and blessed Mary. Mary's response was a song of praise and worship to the God who had shown such grace to them both. Mary's journey to Judea was more than just a geographical journey from one town to another; it was also a journey from wonderment and confusion to joyful affirmation of God's goodness.

24 May

Immanuel – God with us

Isaiah 7

'The virgin will be with child and will give birth to a son, and will call him Immanuel.' (v.14)

'Immanuel' speaks of the amazing truth of God being 'with us' on this earth, in the form of His Son, Jesus. He is always with us. And how we need Him in these times of 'wars and rumours of wars'; how we need Him if we're to stand any chance of being righteous, loving, and holy as He is holy. God is still with us, through ups and downs, to discipline, laugh with, comfort or exhort us. Isn't that amazing!

9 August

Mary's journey to Bethlehem

Luke 2:4–7,15–20

'… *Mary treasured up all these things and pondered them in her heart.' (v.19)*

In making that long and uncomfortable journey in the final stages of pregnancy, Mary matured. Now she had to draw on inner strength from God Himself and trust Joseph in practical matters. Right out of her 'comfort zone' and without her mother for help with the birth, she was cut off from all she had known and relied on for security up to that point. But God's grace and provision proved sufficient.

25 May

Holy, holy, holy is the Lord

Isaiah 6:1–4

'In the year that King Uzziah died, I saw the Lord seated on a throne, high and exalted, and the train of his robe filled the temple. Above him were seraphs, each with six wings: With two wings they covered their faces, with two they covered their feet, and with two they were flying. And they were calling to one another: "Holy, holy, holy is the Lord Almighty; the whole earth is full of his glory." At the sound of their voices the doorposts and thresholds shook and the temple was filled with smoke.'

8 August

Mary's journey to the Temple

Luke 2:22–38

'Simeon took the child in his arms and gave thanks to God.' (v.28, GNB)

As God-fearing Jews, Mary and Joseph would naturally fulfil their spiritual duty by journeying to Jerusalem to present their child to God. Sometimes we long for God to speak to us in special ways and occasionally He does so; more often, however, He speaks through others who love Him as, like Mary and Joseph, we seek to fulfil our spiritual obligations and as we routinely offer the 'sacrifice of praise'.

26 May

Holiness

Isaiah 6

'... they were calling to one another: "Holy, holy, holy is the LORD Almighty ..."' (v.3)

What is holiness? God is more wholly righteous than we ever could be. Our right response is to repent, to mourn, to feel that we deserve to die. But while Isaiah needed the agony of a burning coal on his lips, we can draw near to God's throne boldly, 'in full assurance of faith' because Jesus has opened 'a new and living way' through suffering and dying in our place (Heb. 10:19–22).

Mary's journey to Egypt

Matthew 2:1–18

' "Get up," he said, "take the child and his mother and escape to Egypt …" ' (v.13)

Mary found herself fleeing by night to Egypt and becoming a refugee in a land where she didn't speak the language, where Jews weren't especially welcome and where she had neither the props of a shared faith and culture nor the support of the friends she'd doubtless made in Bethlehem. At such times, like Mary, we too can know that God has everything in hand and will guide and protect us.

27 May

'Bad is good'

Isaiah 5:20–30

'Woe to those who call evil good and good evil … who put bitter for sweet and sweet for bitter.' (v.20)

This passage could have been written for our century. It's 'wrong', we're told, for a teacher to hug a five-year-old who is distressed. It's 'right' to see how much you can drink in an evening – it proves you're a sociable, fun-loving person without silly inhibitions. Anything can be twisted by those who are sick or evil but God is our guiding North Star among dangers which threaten to wreck humanity.

6 August

Another journey to the Temple

Luke 2:41–52

'... *his mother treasured all these things in her heart.*' (v.51)

nother regular journey to the Temple turned into a further spiritual journey for Mary. Mary's pent-up anxiety and exasperation are wonderfully conveyed, but her son's reply indicated that His journey was beginning to be separate from hers. It is not always easy to 'let go' emotionally or spiritually, either of our natural or 'spiritual' children, but we have to learn to do so, allowing them independence.

28 May

The Gardener

Isaiah 5:1–19

*'What more could have been done for my vineyard …
why did it yield only bad [grapes]?' (v.4)*

Adding 'house to house … till no space is left'
(v.8) was about the rich pushing the poor off
the land. A desperation for alcohol at all hours
(v.11) rings a few bells in our 21st-century 'civilised'
world too. The people have no regard for God (v.12).
Do you sense 'Gardener' God's sadness, for Israel
in Isaiah's time and for our world today? Listen to His
heartbeat. Let it prompt you to pray.

5 August

Our Pentecost journey

Acts 2:1–12

'When the day of Pentecost came, they were all together in one place.' (v.1)

Although we often focus on individual journeys we also celebrate today the start of a communal journey. The disciples, without the physical presence of Jesus but in the power of the Holy Spirit, began to proclaim the gospel. We too are part of that pilgrim church, individuals making up the Body of Christ. We journey with others in that same excitement of living and in the same power of the Holy Spirit.

29 May

Haughty women

Isaiah 3

'The women of Zion are haughty … flirting with their eyes … ornaments jingling …' (v.16)

Many women today worship style and celebrity while others haven't a cup of clean water to give their sick children. There's nothing wrong with looking nice – but there is something very wrong with haughtiness, self-obsession and the use of sex for power. But many other women are truly a delight. Weren't Mother Teresa's wrinkled face and hands beautiful – to rich and poor, black and white, to God *and* humankind?

4 August

Filled with the Holy Spirit

Acts 2:2–4

'Suddenly a sound like the blowing of a violent wind came from heaven and filled the whole house where they were sitting. They saw what seemed to be tongues of fire that separated and came to rest on each of them. All of them were filled with the Holy Spirit and began to speak in other tongues as the Spirit enabled them.'

High places

Isaiah 2

'The arrogance of man … brought low … pride … humbled; the Lord alone will be exalted …' (v.17)

What are the high places in your life? What is worth the most to you? What makes you feel proud, excited? Your house, achievements, clothes, friends, family? Some are good, yet this prophecy says there is room for only one 'highest place' – the 'mountain of the Lord's temple' (v.2). A temple is where a god is worshipped. May we never put God second (or last) but always in the highest place.

3 August

Mary's journey to the cross

John 19:25–27

'When Jesus saw his mother there, and the disciple whom he loved standing near by, he said … "… here is your son" …' (v.26)

Mary's journey had come to the point of seeing her son crucified. Sometimes on our journeys we reach rock-bottom and feel that things cannot get any worse. We may despair, as if we're in a pit from which we can't climb out. Jesus knows. He is there, even if we can't sense His presence. He is there in the darkest hour and He has not abandoned us. He has made provision for us, just as He made provision for Mary.

31 May

Testing times

Isaiah 1

'I reared children and brought them up, but they have rebelled against me.' (v.2)

Just as we couldn't let our two-year-old son trash the house or himself, God couldn't let His beloved people either trash the weak among them – the fatherless and the widows – or revere other gods. Yet He's still willing to reason with them and then, 'If you are willing and obedient, you will eat the best from the land' (v.19). What a picture of His grace's supernatural power and what amazing desire to bless!

Set aside for Jesus

Ephesians 1:1–6

'For he chose us in him before the creation of the world to be holy and blameless in his sight.' (v.4)

So often women feel that they aren't very special; that they don't matter or they've got nothing to contribute. Well, if that's you, then today's verses are just for you, in fact, the whole of Ephesians is just for you! God has chosen to show favour and make it available to all humans – if they will just reach out and receive it. God has chosen us all – the key question is: have we chosen Him?

White as snow

Isaiah 1:16–19

'Wash and make yourselves clean. Take your evil deeds out of my sight! Stop doing wrong, learn to do right! Seek justice, encourage the oppressed. Defend the cause of the fatherless, plead the case of the widow. "Come now, let us reason together," says the Lord. "Though your sins are like scarlet, they shall be as white as snow; though they are red as crimson, they shall be like wool. If you are willing and obedient, you will eat the best from the land …'

Redemption through His blood

Ephesians 1:7–10

'In him we have redemption … the forgiveness of sins in accordance with the riches of God's grace …' (v.7)

Redemption isn't a word that we often use today, but in the Bible the idea of redeeming things was quite common. To redeem something basically meant that if something that had initially belonged to you had fallen into someone else's hands, you could, under certain conditions, negotiate a price by which you could buy it back, no strings attached. The price for us was the life of Jesus, God's Son.

Insights from Isaiah

Isaiah 1:1

'The vision concerning Judah and Jerusalem that Isaiah son of Amoz saw during the reigns of Uzziah, Jotham, Ahaz and Hezekiah, kings of Judah.' (v.1)

saiah's writing is the pinnacle of Old Testament prophecy, poetry and theology. We're in the Bronze Age, 740–701 BC, reading the prophet Isaiah's visions concerning middle-eastern kingdoms and people. Yet they not only speak to us in the 21st century AD, they're scarily relevant. In some ways that's understandable – God hasn't changed, nor, essentially, have people.

Signed, sealed and delivered

Ephesians 1: 11 – 14

'Having believed, you were marked in him with a seal, the promised Holy Spirit …' (v.13b)

When the Father bought us back from the kingdom of darkness we did not become a possession to live in fear of Him, but we became His adopted children with the same rights as His own Son – heirs and heiresses in the kingdom of God. God seals the agreement between Himself and His adopted children by filling them with His Holy Spirit as a guarantee and reassurance that His promises will be fulfilled.

3 June

Heaven and earth

Revelation 21:1–4

*'… prepared as a bride beautifully dressed for
her husband.' (v.2)*

God created a beautiful world full of stunning
colours, breathtaking vistas and amazing
creatures. The bride is 'prepared' and
'beautifully dressed'. Just like everything else God
made, heaven will be a place of astonishing beauty. It's
compared to a bride at her most beautiful. If you cannot
visualise heaven, if it all seems remote, connect it with
that first act of creation and magnify it a thousand-fold.

30 July

Enlighten the eyes of my heart

Ephesians 1: 15–23

'I keep asking that … the glorious Father, may give you the Spirit of wisdom and revelation …' (v.17)

Until we have the gift of the Holy Spirit in our lives it is impossible for our earthbound senses to begin to perceive the boundlessness of God's love for us, the incomparably great power that has been released in our lives and the spiritual riches that are ours in Christ if we are willing to appropriate them. The Spirit begins to enlighten the eyes of our heart and helps us to know Jesus better.

4 June

Heaven on earth

Ephesians 4:2–16

'… so that the body of Christ may be built up.' (v.12)

The Church is meant to be a foretaste of heaven, a glowing, enticing example to outsiders who'll be drawn in by its attractiveness. But I suspect for many of us church is the place where you get hurt. And Paul knows it. Here, yet again, he has to urge the believers to stop behaving badly. The Church is not Christ's toy, it is His pleasure. And it's my job, not someone else's, to make it just like heaven.

29 July

Don't bury your talent

Ephesians 2:1–10

'For we are God's workmanship, created in Christ Jesus to do good works, which God prepared in advance for us to do.' (v.10)

Many people are thrilled with the idea that we are saved by faith in God's grace, and not by works. But faith that doesn't show itself in action isn't much good to anyone. Have you asked the Holy Spirit to enlighten you as to what it is He has planned for you to *do* by the grace you have received? Each of us has some particular flair for something. What's yours? How can you use it for God's glory?

5 June

Really useful

2 Timothy 3:14–17

'All Scripture is God-breathed and is useful for teaching, rebuking, correcting and training …' (v.16)

Scripture assumes that we need correction and rebuke just as much as we need teaching and training. This passage tells us a bit more about why God wrote to us; why His words are so important. The whole of the Bible is intended to shape our thinking. Our thought patterns need realigning. As we read it, He breathes truth from the page into our minds and hearts, for it empowers way beyond mere human words.

28 July

Grace – God's Riches At Christ's Expense

Ephesians 2:4–9

'But because of his great love for us, God, who is rich in mercy, made us alive with Christ even when we were dead in transgressions – it is by grace you have been saved. And God raised us up with Christ and seated us with him in the heavenly realms in Christ Jesus, in order that in the coming ages he might show the incomparable riches of his grace, expressed in his kindness to us in Christ Jesus. For it is by grace you have been saved, through faith – and this not from yourselves, it is the gift of God – not by works, so that no-one can boast.'

6 June

What are you reading?

1 Chronicles 16:8–25

'Remember the wonders he has done …' (v.12)

'OK, I want to start with a quick survey today,' said my pastor husband. 'How many of you have ever read any book cover to cover?' Every hand in the church went up. 'Now, how many of you have read the Bible cover to cover?' And the embarrassed multitude slid lower in their pews. The Bible is about real ordinary people just like us. So why do we hesitate to read what we say is so important?

27 July

In on everything now

Ephesians 2: 11 – 13

'… in Christ Jesus you who once were far away have been brought near through the blood of Christ.' (v.13)

No one likes to think they are being left out of something and when we *are* involved, it can be so easy to forget what it is like to be ostracised and how wonderful the feeling was when we were first included. We must never take grace for granted and what the Father achieved in Christ – it took the blood of Jesus to include us in, to bring us near and make us part of His chosen people.

The Spirit's power

1 Corinthians 2:1–16

'... with a demonstration of the Spirit's power ...' (v.4)

The Holy Spirit is constantly busy, influencing Christians to be effective servants of God, connecting heaven to earth, bringing the very Spirit of Jesus Himself into your life, showing you what God is thinking, giving you discernment so you can sort out truth and reality from lies. You notice the difference when the Spirit is empowering you. How we dare put Him in the background, I can't imagine!

26 July

The Holy Spirit's dwelling

Ephesians 2:14–22

'And in him you too are being built together to become a dwelling in which God lives by his Spirit.' (v.22)

What we need to remember is that every believer has the same 'spiritual glue' inside them that sticks us all together in Christ; it's not the wrapper that counts, but what's inside. One reason why we won't relate to other Christians is because we are frightened of them, but if we dare show them the love of Christ, we will find that even Christians we find outwardly awkward contain the same Spirit as we do.

8 June

A generous gift

Titus 3:3–7

'At one time we too were foolish, disobedient, deceived and enslaved by all kinds of passions and pleasures. We lived in malice and envy, being hated and hating one another. But when the kindness and love of God our Saviour appeared, he saved us, not because of righteous things we had done, but because of his mercy. He saved us through the washing of rebirth and renewal by the Holy Spirit, whom he poured out on us generously through Jesus Christ our Saviour, so that, having been justified by his grace, we might become heirs having the hope of eternal life.'

25 July

You'd better believe it!

Ephesians 3:1–6

'For this reason I, Paul, the prisoner of Christ Jesus for the sake of you Gentiles –' (v.1)

The message of God's grace is so unbelievable that Paul tells the Ephesians they'd better believe it! As proof, he reminds them of his personal encounter with Jesus and that he is in prison because he has dared to preach this message to Jewish and non-Jewish people alike. He would not have accepted this fate if he weren't convinced in his heart by the revelation of the Spirit that all this was true.

9 June

Blasé

Titus 3:4–7

*'…the Holy Spirit, whom he poured out on us
generously through Jesus Christ our Saviour …'*
(vv.5–6)

For me, becoming a Christian was a gigantic,
relief-giving, emotional step into the kingdom of
God. Yet, as the years have rolled by, sometimes
my awe has decreased. Such blasé Christian living is
no good. I need to let my excited teenage daughter
and her enthusiastic evangelism shift my middle-aged
complacent balance. God *pours* out; I don't have the
right to *trickle* only a little back.

24 July

Less than the least of all

Ephesians 3:7–9

'Although I am less than the least of all God's people, this grace was given me: to preach …' (v.8)

Maybe, like a lot of women, you think you haven't got any abilities to be proud of! Whatever we think we can or can't do, if we humbly give everything in our life to God, He can use the abilities He has given us in ways beyond our imagination, to fulfil all the things He planned ahead of time for us to do. Let's ask God to use what we've got, giving Jesus all the glory for the results.

10 June

What's He for?

Romans 8:5–11

'… the mind controlled by the Spirit is
life and peace.' (v.6)

What does Scripture say about the Holy Spirit? Not only does He influence thoughts, He also gives life which is not some metaphorical life but 'life to your mortal bodies'. He is essential to Christian living. He breathes in strength to us to enable us to live beyond what might be expected, just as the raising of Jesus was beyond what was expected. That's how powerful the Spirit can be in your life!

23 July

Freedom and confidence

Ephesians 3: 10–13

'In him and through faith in him we may approach God with freedom and confidence.' (v.12)

I don't know what having four children did to me, but somehow I lost my confidence and, subsequently, my freedom! Reminding yourself that you are a daughter of the King is the first step to regaining the confidence you may have lost. We are valuable and useful to God; that realisation gives us the freedom and confidence to follow where His Spirit leads as He begins to open up new horizons for us.

11 June

By faith

Hebrews 11:1–19

'… they were longing for a better country – a
heavenly one.' (v.16)

Have I matured in character, in grace, in
pleasing Him in Christian service? Or has
faith become learning without living? Is there
a faith gap? The gap must be closed. This passage
shows what others have done in faith. If I don't believe
enough to *do*, then, put simply, *in that area* I'm not a
believer. If I believe in Jesus for salvation, why won't I
live it out in every area?

22 July

The measure of God's fullness

Ephesians 3: 14–21

'... the measure of all the fulness of God.' (v.19)

On a Pacific coral island I was surrounded by miles of empty ocean, the unending blue sky and I knew the sea floor dropped off at least a mile just feet from the beach. I reflected on the chorus that God's love is wider than the ocean, higher than the heavens and deeper than the sea. That day I gained a whole new perspective of the measure of God's fulness and the dimensions of Christ's love for us.

12 June

The good news for now

Matthew 6:19–34

'Are you not much more valuable than they?' (v.26)

A gospel that gets me to heaven tomorrow is great but I desperately need a gospel that works today as well. Yet today we choose to worry about things. But perhaps we haven't noticed *why* we don't need to worry. The reason is that we're valuable to God. His fatherhood and love commit Him to providing all we need. Our relationship of trust makes all the difference to the way we can live now.

21 July

The love of Christ

Ephesians 3:14–19

'For this reason I kneel before the Father, from whom his whole family in heaven and on earth derives its name. I pray that out of his glorious riches he may strengthen you with power through his Spirit in your inner being, so that Christ may dwell in your hearts through faith. And I pray that you, being rooted and established in love, may have power, together with all the saints, to grasp how wide and long and high and deep is the love of Christ, and to know this love that surpasses knowledge – that you may be filled to the measure of all the fulness of God.'

13 June

Getting the centre right

John 15: 1–17

'Now remain in my love.' (v.9)

Warren was a most unlikeable child and yet his mother actually loved him and talked about him as if she didn't see his obvious deficiencies! That's the difference love makes. Many Christians base their faith and view of others on keeping rules. And while God's world is law-based – that's the way He made it so it would run right – lovingly knitted in closeness to God is the key to successful Christian living.

20 July

A life worthy of the calling

Ephesians 4:1–6

'Make every effort to keep the unity of the Spirit through the bond of peace.' (v.3)

Living for Jesus is a minute-by-minute conscious choice; a choice to praise rather than blame, a choice to share rather than snatch, a choice to help rather than hinder. Eventually those choices become habits and reflect Christ's love to others. The world sees the reality of our Christian faith by our love for each other. How can you make a practical effort to show that unity of the Spirit?

What God wants

Luke 7:36–50

'... *she loved much.*' (v.47)

What response does God want from humankind? What does He really want? I expect most of us would say, 'To believe'. And that is surely true. Yet, somehow the word 'believe' suggests mental assent, merely what I *think* about something. The woman's sins are forgiven, not because of what she thought, but because she loved responsively. Perhaps we need to reorient our theology to what Jesus applauds.

19 July

Grace as Christ apportioned

Ephesians 4:7–13

'But to each one of us grace has been given as Christ apportioned it.' (v.7)

We women are so funny! I once heard a pastor's wife, who is an excellent speaker, saying how she had felt threatened by another woman's culinary skills. I had to laugh, because I *can* cook, but feel threatened by women who find speaking at meetings easy! It has been a long journey, but I have learned the hard way that there is no point comparing myself with other people because we all have different roles.

15 June

But I tell you

Matthew 5:38–44

'You have heard that it was said, "Eye for eye, and tooth for tooth." But I tell you, Do not resist an evil person. If someone strikes you on the right cheek, turn to him the other also. And if someone wants to sue you and take your tunic, let him have your cloak as well. If someone forces you to go one mile, go with him two miles. Give to the one who asks you, and do not turn away from the one who wants to borrow from you.

You have heard that it was said, "Love your neighbour and hate your enemy." But I tell you: Love your enemies and pray for those who persecute you.'

18 July

Time to grow up

Ephesians 4:14–16

'Then we will no longer be infants … blown here and there by every wind of teaching …' (v.14a)

Knowing we are daughters of the King, understanding the riches of our spiritual inheritance and serving the Lord with the abilities He has given us is part of growing up as a Christian. A wise Christian woman has a mature faith that builds up her spiritual life, and the lives of those around her, and is strong enough to resist every wind of deceitful novelty teaching.

16 June

What should I do?

Matthew 5:27–48

'You have heard that it was said, "Love your neighbour and hate your enemy." But I tell you: Love your enemies and pray for those who persecute you.' (vv.43–44)

Am I living it right? The Christian life, I mean. Does the Bible mean what it says or have I submitted to the culture all around me. My conscience is soothed because, by and large, nobody else around me is living all that radically. I don't mean to condemn anyone other than myself, but I certainly don't engage in too much coat-giving, cheek-turning, blessing of enemies.

17 July

The ultimate makeover

Ephesians 4:17–24

'You were taught … to put off your old self … to be made new in the attitude of your minds …' (vv.22–23)

The current craze on TV for lifestyle makeover shows often only deal with the visible symptoms and don't really address the heart of the problem. It's like the man who prayed for God to 'get rid of the cobwebs in my life' only to be told that it was his own responsibility to kill the spider! The sort of change Paul spoke of is initiated on the inside of our lives, in our hearts and our minds.

17 June

Someone to keep the agreement

Hebrews 9: 11 – 18

'… Christ is the mediator of a new covenant …' (v.15)

The whole of the rest of the Bible after Genesis 3 is what God did to rescue the doomed covenant agreement and still keep the concept of covenant love at the heart of things. Instead of turning His back on us, since we failed to meet our side of the deal, God had a way of restoring us into a relationship with Him again. Jesus would obey the demands of the covenant on our behalf. He would do what we had endlessly failed to do.

Taking out the trash

Ephesians 4:25–31

'Get rid of all bitterness, rage and anger ... Be kind and compassionate to one another, forgiving each other ...' (vv.31–32)

I began my married life with an unspoken burden of bitterness towards the Church. I had wanted an academic career, but had to sacrifice that and take a job so that my husband would qualify for support through his ministerial training. I eventually became very depressed but after prayer and counselling I got rid of all my anger and bitterness. I was able to forgive, and asked for forgiveness – and was miraculously healed.

18 June

With this ring

Hosea 3:1–5; 11:1–9

'Love her as the LORD loves the Israelites ...' (3:1)

For any relationship to work there has to be the moment when you drop all others and keep to one only. That was why God went for covenant relationships. It's the commitment of a definite agreement that actually provides the basis of such a safe world. You know where you are with God. He's put it in writing. Even when we are unfaithful God agonises in His love that He cannot bear to withhold from us.

15 July

The thin red line

Ephesians 5:1–6

'But among you there must not be even a hint of sexual immorality …' (v.3)

We are to live a life of love, but Paul qualifies this by saying '*there must not even be a hint of sexual immorality*' among believers. It is good to err on the side of caution; the smallest of gestures can be misinterpreted. We can ensure that we know where the line is drawn in relation to our own weaknesses and our knowledge of other people's weaknesses, and make sure we stay within those boundaries.

19 June

Commitment of another kind

Isaiah 46:3–13

'I have made you and I will carry you ...' (v.4)

The universe has been made. Now what? Leave it all to roll along like an unmanned spaceship and wait to see what happens? Stop and think for a moment, instead, of the whole stretch of Scripture and the history of humanity. From beginning to end it shouts, 'I am involved. I am interested.' The scope of God's involvement and commitment to you is: 'I have' 'I am' and 'I will' – past, present and future.

14 July

Live a life of love

Ephesians 5:1–4

'Be imitators of God, therefore, as dearly loved children and live a life of love, just as Christ loved us and gave himself up for us as a fragrant offering and sacrifice to God. But among you there must not be even a hint of sexual immorality, or of any kind of impurity, or of greed, because these are improper for God's holy people. Nor should there be obscenity, foolish talk or coarse joking, which are out of place, but rather thanksgiving.'

20 June

Hearing from heaven

Matthew 7:7–12

'For everyone who asks receives …' (v.8)

Dallas Willard says of God's listening capacity, 'You cannot call upon Jesus Christ or upon God and not be heard.' No words fall on distracted ears, no half-verbalised hopes or agonised cries get overlooked because somebody more important or more interesting is praying at the same moment. It is never, therefore, a waste of time to pray. What is God going to hear you say today?

13 July

Walking in the light

Ephesians 5:7–14

'For you were once darkness, but now you are light in the Lord. Live as children of light …' (v.8)

God doesn't want us to live a lie, but to walk in truth and light – finding out what pleases Him and what needs to be cleared away. The way I measure if I am walking in the light rather than lurking in shades of grey is to ask myself, 'Would I mind if it was shouted from the roof tops?' or more particularly, 'How would I feel if Jesus was right there next to me?' Remember, Jesus is always ready to forgive.

21 June

The God who loves to talk

1 Samuel 3:1–10

'Speak, Lord, for your servant is listening.' (v.9)

God didn't just make the world; He *spoke* the world into being. It certainly suggests that the idea of speaking is part of the very nature of God. He gave us His 'Word' – all that He has said to mankind – in His Book. Jesus Himself is called 'the Word' and again and again through Scripture we find the phrase 'God said' or 'God spoke'. We have a God who loves to talk and is eager to communicate with us.

Be filled with the Spirit

Ephesians 5:15–20

'Do not get drunk on wine, which leads to debauchery. Instead, be filled with the Spirit.' (v.18)

Alcohol has always been a tricky issue. Many Christians won't drink alcohol – and that's fine; but Paul is not saying a blanket 'don't', he is saying don't look to alcohol for your highs in life, as a means of alleviating stress or finding false courage when you're lacking confidence. Instead God wants us to be filled with the *real* joy and *genuine* confidence that comes from the indwelling of His Spirit.

22 June

Faith in Jesus Christ

Galatians 2:16,19–20

'Know that a man is not justified by observing the law, but by faith in Jesus Christ. So we, too, have put our faith in Christ Jesus that we may be justified by faith in Christ and not by observing the law, because by observing the law no-one will be justified … For through the law I died to the law so that I might live for God. I have been crucified with Christ and I no longer live, but Christ lives in me. The life I live in the body, I live by faith in the Son of God, who loved me and gave himself for me.'

Submission

Ephesians 5:21–27

'Submit to one another out of reverence for Christ.' (v.21)

Paul is actually saying we should be accountable to each other because we flow in the same Holy Spirit, whether married or single. So, women, don't get hung up on the *submission* word; it doesn't mean mindless obedience to male domination, but mutual accountability. *Submission* (v.21) and *love* (v.25) are actually the same thing – both involve selfless sacrifice and constant reference to each other.

23 June

For me

Galatians 2: 11–21

'... the Son of God, who loved me and gave himself
for me' (v.20).

Isn't the Bible all about believing the right things and signing on the dotted line of assent? No – really it's about relationship. The truth is that this loving, giving, involved, creative, communicating God wants a response. How much have we received without response? How much love and care do we take for granted because it comes week in week out? All that He does and says is for us – no one else!

Selfless self-interest

Ephesians 5:28–33

'… no-one ever hated his own body, but he feeds and cares for it, just as Christ does the church …' (v.29)

Husbands should nurture their wives and care for them. In a culture where women were treated like possessions and slaves, what Paul was advocating was quite revolutionary. Usually men would take the best part of the food, and women and children would eat what was left. It was quite a thing to suggest that a man should give his wife the portion that he would preferably have required for himself!

24 June

Giving things away

John 14:1–4

'I am going there to prepare a place for you.' (v.2)

God's handcrafted piece for us was the world. He made it carefully; then gave it away. 'The highest heavens belong to the LORD, but the earth he has given to man,' says Psalm 115:16. Making and giving, making and giving; that's the pattern that God follows. Now, as today's passage says, Jesus is still busy making something for us. He's working on our next world, on heaven.

9 July

Parents and children

Ephesians 6:1–4

'... do not exasperate your children ... bring them up in the training and instruction of the Lord.' (v.4)

If I thought three toddlers and a baby was difficult, three teenagers and a seven-year-old are much worse! I never appreciated how exasperated and exasperating I could become in return. I try to remember that mutual accountability that flows from a life in the Spirit demands unconditional love; but it is the parent that has to start the ball rolling and keep it rolling, despite what the child does.

Holy One

Psalm 99:1–9

'The Lord reigns, let the nations tremble ...' (v.1)

When God gave Moses directions for the tabernacle, He made a separate area, the Holy of Holies, to demarcate holiness from mess, contamination and sin. Holiness separates itself from sin, like we'd separate ourselves from plague. The nations tremble because they have had an awesome sight of God's holiness. In us, it should produce awe, worship and gratitude that we can approach the Holy of Holies in person.

8 July

A will to work

Ephesians 6:5–9

'Serve wholeheartedly, as if you were serving the Lord, not men ...' (v.7)

All women work – whether in offices, shops and schools, or from home looking after children or running small businesses. And we all have housework to do! There is no avoiding it – we all work and have responsibilities – we get tired, and find ourselves asking the question, 'What am I doing all this for?' For the Christian, the answer is easy – everything we do we are, or should be, doing for Jesus.

26 June

World-maker

Genesis 1:1–27

'In the beginning God created …' (v.1)

When we read Genesis, we tend to move quickly past those opening five words to the detail of everything that God actually made. This time, stop for a moment and focus on this, God's first recorded action. Think of all the words which could be used to describe God's creative powers: invent, build, construct, form, make, shape, craft. Which makes you see God in a new light?

The world of work

Ephesians 6:5–6,8–9

'Slaves, obey your earthly masters with respect and fear, and with sincerity of heart, just as you would obey Christ. Obey them not only to win their favour when their eye is on you, but like slaves of Christ, doing the will of God from your heart … because you know that the Lord will reward everyone for whatever good he does, whether he is slave or free. And masters, treat your slaves in the same way. Do not threaten them, since you know that he who is both their Master and yours is in heaven, and there is no favouritism with him.'

27 June

Three into one does go

John 14: 15–30

'… I am in my Father, and you are in me, and I am in you.' (v.20)

How can He be going and still here? The answer is that Jesus' place will be taken by the Holy Spirit. His followers will see Him as the Counsellor sent by the Father, so God's personal presence will always be with them. One of the most striking things about today's passage is the interwoven co-operation and harmony of the Father, Son and Holy Spirit. Love and intimacy are at the heart of Godhead.

6 July

Be strong in the Lord

Ephesians 6:10–12

*'Finally, be strong in the Lord and in his mighty power.
Put on the full armour of God …' (vv.10–11a)*

God wants us to be strong; not with the grit and determination that come from our inner self but in the strength of His power. Being strong in the Lord is not just about being filled with power on the inside, but about being prepared on the outside. That's why we are encouraged to put on the armour of God. What do you put on first in the morning – your slippers or your armour?

The myth of empty space

Psalm 139: 1–18

'Where can I flee from your presence?' (v.7)

In this psalm David realises – not always with a sense of comfort – that God is everywhere. He talks of fleeing (v.7) and hiding (v.11) but it's futile, the God who has always been is also everywhere. We live in His universe, His place and nowhere is without His presence. Wherever you are right now, He is there, fully and in person. As Dallas Willard says, 'Space is inhabited by God' – all of it!

5 July

The full armour of God

Ephesians 6: 13– 17

'Therefore put on the full armour of God, so that when the day of evil comes, you may be able to stand your ground …' (v.13a)

Our spiritual armour protects our two most sensitive and vital parts – our hearts and our heads. These are the parts where I feel women, who have a tendency to need reassurance and affirmation, are especially vulnerable. The heart is the seat of our desires, and the head the seat of our thoughts. Both control the way we behave. We protect our hearts with God's righteousness and our heads with knowing His Word.

29 June

God's revelation

1 Corinthians 2:10–13

'But God has revealed it to us by his Spirit. The Spirit searches all things, even the deep things of God. For who among men knows the thoughts of a man except the man's spirit within him? In the same way no-one knows the thoughts of God except the Spirit of God. We have not received the spirit of the world but the Spirit who is from God, that we may understand what God has freely given us. This is what we speak, not in words taught us by human wisdom but in words taught by the Spirit, expressing spiritual truths in spiritual words.'

4 July

Praying in the Spirit

Ephesians 6: 18–24

'And pray in the Spirit on all occasions … be alert and always keep on praying for all the saints.' (v.18)

Spiritual armour is not just for defence but also attack; we have the sword of the Spirit, God's written Word, which we can use as a defensive and an offensive weapon, but our major offensive weapon is praying in the Spirit. Praying in the Spirit happens on those occasions we let God direct our prayers, rather than just coming to Him with a list of needs and anxieties; when we allow the Holy Spirit to direct what we pray about and how we pray.

Beyond imagination

1 Corinthians 2:1–16

'No eye has seen, no ear has heard, no mind has conceived what God has prepared for those who love him' (v.9).

Baby Jessica's universe currently begins and ends with parts of Glasgow! I suspect we are similarly limited here on earth. God You're bigger and beyond, You're more and You're greater, You're here and everywhere, You're altogether other. But one day we will step off this earth into God's presence, into an unfathomable new awareness of what we could never have imagined in our wildest dreams.

3 July

The big picture

Philippians 2:1–11

'… *he humbled himself and became obedient* …' (v.8)

There is a plan into which I am meant to fit; a bigger picture than I currently see. If I focus on me and only me, then I become a lost Christian, sickly and disorientated, not sure what matters or why. I need to stand back and look at the big picture of what faith's all about and how I fit in. If Jesus, the Lord of the universe, humbled Himself, isn't it about time I did too?

Before the beginning

John 1:1–14

'In the beginning was the Word, and the Word was with God, and the Word was God.' (v.1)

When was the beginning? We tend to think of creation as the start, simply because our minds can only cope with what we can see and find evidence for. But God – Father, Son and Holy Spirit – existed before there was anything else. This is the God we worship. The God who always has been and who always will be. And this God, out of the aeons of time, came to dwell with us and call us His children.

2 July

National Distributors

UK: (and countries not listed below)
CWR, Waverley Abbey House, Waverley Lane, Farnham, Surrey GU9 8EP.
Tel: (01252) 784700 Outside UK (44) 1252 784700

AUSTRALIA: CMC Australasia, PO Box 519, Belmont, Victoria 3216.
Tel: (03) 5241 3288 Fax: (03) 5241 3290

CANADA: David C Cook Distribution Canada, PO Box 98, 55 Woodslee Avenue,
Paris, Ontario N3L 3E5. Tel: 1800 263 2664

GHANA: Challenge Enterprises of Ghana, PO Box 5723, Accra.
Tel: (021) 222437/223249 Fax: (021) 226227

HONG KONG: Cross Communications Ltd, 1/F, 562A Nathan Road, Kowloon.
Tel: 2780 1188 Fax: 2770 6229

INDIA: Crystal Communications, 10-3-18/4/1, East Marredpalli, Secunderabad
– 500026, Andhra Pradesh. Tel/Fax: (040) 27737145

KENYA: Keswick Books and Gifts Ltd, PO Box 10242, Nairobi.
Tel: (02) 331692/226047 Fax: (02) 728557

MALAYSIA: Salvation Book Centre (M) Sdn Bhd, 23 Jalan SS 2/64, 47300
Petaling Jaya, Selangor.
Tel: (03) 78766411/78766797 Fax: (03) 78757066/78756360

NEW ZEALAND: CMC Australasia, PO Box 303298, North Harbour, Auckland
0751. Tel: 0800 449 408 Fax: 0800 449 049

NIGERIA: FBFM, Helen Baugh House, 96 St Finbarr's College Road, Akoka,
Lagos. Tel: (01) 7747429/4700218/825775/827264

PHILIPPINES: OMF Literature Inc, 776 Boni Avenue, Mandaluyong City.
Tel: (02) 531 2183 Fax: (02) 531 1960

SINGAPORE: Alby Commercial Enterprises Pte Ltd, 95 Kallang Avenue #04-00, AIS Industrial Building, 339420. Tel: (65) 629 27238 Fax: (65) 629 27235

SOUTH AFRICA: Struik Christian Books, 80 MacKenzie Street, PO Box 1144, Cape Town 8000. Tel: (021) 462 4360 Fax: (021) 461 3612

SRI LANKA: Christombu Publications (Pvt) Ltd, Bartleet House, 65 Braybrooke Place, Colombo 2. Tel: (9411) 2421073/2447665

TANZANIA: CLC Christian Book Centre, PO Box 1384, Mkwepu Street, Dar es Salaam. Tel/Fax: (022) 2119439

USA: David C Cook Distribution Canada, PO Box 98, 55 Woodslee Avenue, Paris, Ontario N3L 3E5, Canada. Tel: 1800 263 2664

ZIMBABWE: Word of Life Books (Pvt) Ltd, Christian Media Centre, 8 Aberdeen Road, Avondale, PO Box A480 Avondale, Harare. Tel: (04) 333355 or 091301188

For email addresses, visit the CWR website: www.cwr.org.uk

CWR is a Registered Charity – Number 294387

CWR is a Limited Company registered in England – Registration Number 1990308